KEYS TO MOVE FROM

WAY TRUTH LIFE

GREG HENDRICKS

FOREWORD BY KRIS VALLOTTON

Way Truth Life by GREG HENDRICKS

Copyright © 2022

Special discounts are available on quantity purchases by corporations, associations, and others. Orders by US trade bookstores and wholesalers—for details, contact the author vie the website above.

ISBN: 978-1-7332548-8-5

ACKNOWLEDGMENTS

This book would not have been possible without the support, encouragement and love from many I have had the privilege and honor to meet over my lifetime. I have learned from all of you and I am so grateful. I would like to express my deepest gratitude to my mother for always loving me, even when my heart was hard. For showing me how to persevere when things were stacked against me. You truly are one of my greatest inspirations, I love you forever. My sister who has always championed the best in my life to come to pass, and model to me what authentic patience looks like, Love you loads. My wife who has loved me unconditionally and has been my best friend and life companion. You are my blessing from God. You make me a better man, and our family a greater unit!

My wife's family, thank you for being patient with me as we have both grown together over the years. Love you all very deeply.

Lastly, my 3 amazing children Kaleb, Bryden, Nylah. You are and will always be my greatest treasures in life! Dream big, Love well and PRAY always. My deepest desire is that you love and follow God all your living days. I love you with everything I am.

FOREWORD

In the pages, you are about to read Greg transparently invites you into the complexities of battling to find the great prize of living in the Truth of your identity. Identity is one of the most pressing issues of the day. We are living in the most fatherless generation in history! Children are growing up in homes with unstable beams and cracked foundations, left to battle the storms of life without the provision they need, the protection of a man, and promotion into their destinies. The side effects of this are apparent in culture, leaving the world to navigate the challenges of a generation toggling the flame of an identity crisis.

Even if you have not personally weathered the war of fatherlessness in your own life, there have more than likely been challenges and circumstances that have waged bloodshed on your true identity. This is one of the obvious tactics of the enemy; as he takes moments of failure, rejection, or pain in our life and convinces us that this will be our destiny. These little lies are planted deep in the core of our being until they take root and become a forest of deception; they begin to affect the way we move forward and make decisions. Suddenly, we are not free from the shame and evil schemes of the enemy, but rather sucked deep into its weeds. But, this isn't the life we're intended to live. The truth is, the God of the universe sent His only Son so we could live free from the evil plans of the enemy.

Fatherlessness is a personal part of my story, and even though I am well into my sixties, the loss of my father is something I still think about most days. I'd propose one of the greatest gifts a father gives his children is a sense of identity. But, I know it to be true that our greatest source of identity is not limited to our earthly father, rather we have a Heavenly Father who has spoken the truth of who we are since the beginning of time. He's wrapped our physical being around His dreams and destiny of who we would be in this day and age. Greg Hendricks is a man that has walked the road of great courage to search and find His identity in Christ. As you embark on reading this book you will be filled with immense expectation for what living in the way, the truth, and the life could do for your world. As Greg says in his book "Overcoming the lies that we've believed or been told about ourselves will lead us to our true identity." I could not agree more. In order to allow the truth of God to be rooted deeply, we have to uproot the lies of the enemy that have been taking up space. In these pages, you'll be given keys for overcoming victimhood and dismantling the lies of the enemy so you can live in victory.

Kris Vallotton
Author of POVERTY, RICHES & WEALTH & DESTINED TO WIN
www.krisvallotton.com

CONTENTS

INTRODUCTION

As a former professional basketball player, I thought I had it all. I thought my life had meaning, purpose, and value. However, one day, that all came unexpectedly crashing down. I felt beat up and beat down by my circumstances and the world. I had achieved a level of success—being the first in my family to go to college, then moving on to play professional sports and coach at a professional level—but once that was over, I was back home working a normal job, and I was feeling empty, anxious, adrift, and depressed. I was in an emotional tailspin and felt totally lost.

Growing up with few resources and without a father had left some big voids in me that I didn't even realize I had, and I was on a downward spiral. Things that others said about me, as well as my own assumptions about myself, haunted and tormented me, leading to uncontrollable anger, a severe lack of self-worth, and lots of lying. This road brought me dangerously close to losing everything that mattered to me. I was ready to give up.

If our past alone is what dictates our future, there is no hope for most of us. I know this because I thought that way for a long time, and it was shaping my narrative daily. My past could have dictated that I turned out to be bitter, angry, empty, an absent father, living on the street, or addicted to drugs. But the message of this book— the invitation I want to extend to you—is that your past does not have to dictate what your future can be. There is hope for you!

After searching my whole life, I finally found the way I should go, the truth about myself, and the life I was always meant to live. What's beautiful about this is that you can find it too!

This book is about the journey I've been on and the lessons I've learned along the way. I've gone from being fatherless on this earth, with unlimited questions and a limited future, to not only having my questions answered but finding out that my future has impactful potential and promise. It is a journey that's helped me understand my true identity and establish a foundation from which I could grow a powerful and meaningful life. I finally found a way to receive love and break off the labels that I had lived under while I was growing up.

So how about you? Have you allowed any labels or assumptions to shape your life or limit your destiny? Have circumstances or other people's opinions created a narrative which have impacted your journey in life? I wrote this book because I want to empower you to discover that there is hope for your growth and destiny in life.I want to share with you some lessons and key principles I've learned along my journey. I hope it will repair any heartache you have and give you insight to avoid potential pain on the horizon.

The only thing I ask is that you keep an open mind and heart as you read. That you push past whatever assumptions, biases, and preconceived notions you may have, as sometimes these are the very things that can hold us back! That you really consider how you might push past that threshold into your greatest life.

In discovering the truths you are about to read, I was able to reshape the narrative of my life and go from victim to victor. I am excited for you to go on this journey with me. My hope is that you receive some tools to help you discover breakthroughs for your life as well.

Let's go!

CHAPTER

one

{ Overcoming
Our Environment }

There is no question that people who grow up in some kinds of environments can have advantages over others. We see that play out through the schools our children attend, the resources those environments provide, and the opportunities they afford later on. Having played basketball professionally and having coached at the high school level, I witnessed this on a daily basis. If you have the opportunity to attend a major university on an athletic scholarship, or even get the chance to go to a high school in a nice neighborhood, you tend to have access to more resources, better coaching, and more amenities to help really bring out the fullness of your potential as a student athlete. You have access to better education as well. At a government-run school, you tend to have to work with what you are given. Sometimes there are athletic diamonds in the rough that come out of those environments, but usually, those kids have to overcome a whole lot more with a whole lot less.

Have you ever been in a really positive, supportive environment? You usually think more highly of yourself and feel better about yourself in those settings. They are places of hope and opportunity where you can grow as a human being. A positive environment gives you space to explore; you can see that there is more hope and promise for you there, as well as opportunity to go after your dreams. You have clarity. You are free to make mistakes, pick yourself up, dust yourself off, and keep going. It's a place of nurturing and strengthening for your dreams and passions.

If we are not given very many opportunities or exposed to creative ones when we're young, we only obtain a limited amount of perspective, resources, or education. Often, we start to look at unhealthy or unhelpful perspectives or resources to fulfill our desire to grow as a person. We're more susceptible to what people with limited lives or viewpoints think is good for us based on the conclusions they have arrived at through their own experiences. We essentially allow the world to teach us what is right and what

7

is wrong and how to get through hard things—and that can be a very unstable place if it's not grounded on truth. (We'll talk more about that later.)

Our environments impact how we think about ourselves and the opportunities we have to grow. The environment creates the ecosystem of how we see material things, how we view and treat each other, how we handle disagreements, how we view sex, how we receive and give love. All of that is being portrayed to us a certain way, whether through social media, television, movies, entertainment, or other influences. It all impacts us positively or negatively.

Oftentimes, environments dictate our limitations without us even being aware of it. These perceived limitations can stem from others' opinions about us, who they think we are. But they can also come from our own hearts—our fears of dreaming bigger, our thoughts and emotions that go neglected as we grow up. These things can hold us back in life, but they can also be used as springboards to go higher into our callings and destinies.

Understandably some people may be thinking, "Well, this is the only environment I had." I understand that; I grew up in a limited environment, too. *We have to work with what we have.* That was my mentality for many years of my life, and it sucked!

I was raised in a home where the mentality was "make do to get by." We weren't necessarily dirt poor, but we certainly weren't rich. My mother was a Hispanic single mom who worked multiple jobs to take care of me and my sister. I didn't grow up with a male figure in my house, so as a young man of color (both black and Hispanic), it led me, at times, to feel I was struggling to find a sense of grounding and identity, as well as a healthy environment and belonging in life. Part of me was always wondering who I was and where I belonged. I longed to know where I fit in the world, to be accepted by others, and I grew up having *a lot* of questions, fears, doubts, and low self-esteem.

We can feel lost at times, and being grounded in the right things is a crucial starting point for finding hope. Everyone wants to feel they can overcome the pain of their past, but often they don't know how or where to start. They want to experience a sense of "home" wherever they go to feel grounded and stable in an unstable world.

Imagine a storm raging outside, but the house you are in is firm, strong, safe, and even a pleasant place to pass the time until the storm is gone. When the environment is raging around us, we can feel helpless, fearful, and only see despair; we need a home to keep us safe, a shelter from the storm.

Or think of a tree with roots deep in the ground. That tree is less likely to be blown over when storms or high winds come. The deeper the roots, the stronger the tree. Its environment allows it to grow.

The giant redwood trees of California can have interconnected root systems more than a thousand feet deep. They face harsh winds and weather, but they can still survive, grow, and thrive because their deep, connected, vast root systems keep them from falling over or getting uprooted by any kind of wind that blows through.

I didn't grow up in a home where my confidence was built up or where people were really able or willing to model healthy self-esteem. I lived more in survival mode based on not having a dad. My mother had a lot of pain in her life and was always trying to prove her value and worth. Her parents didn't have a strong commitment to each other, and there was no service modeled in the other relationships my mom had growing up.

When her own father left her mother, it deeply hurt my mom. So she was always fighting to get validation from her dad. It showed up as despair, feeling rejected and pushed away; she didn't feel she was loved. It also showed up as a deep need for validation that was passed on to me as well. My grandmother had it, too, and she had a big influence on me as I was growing up. My grandfather left my grandmother for another woman after she did everything to keep their relationship together. So that sense of fatherlessness went back a long way in my family.

Growing up, I felt like a sapling in the middle of a storm with no root system. The things that happened around me impacted me deeply, and I felt I was at the mercy of my situation. Have you ever felt this way? Like you can't get a break long enough to get planted, feel secure, and have peace? It's like everything you've been through, everything that has happened to you, is just beating you up and forcing a false narrative on you, and you don't know how to make it stop long enough to catch your breath. This is one of the most helpless feelings: to feel as if you are trapped with no hope. However, hope is available, as you will read later.

THE BIG MAN

Later in my adult life, I got a chance to see something modeled to me while I was serving as a volunteer assistant coach in the NBA for the Seattle SuperSonics. And what I saw deeply impacted my life!

I became good friends with one of the players on the team. He was a great dude and he worked extremely hard. He had already won an NBA championship with the San Antonio Spurs. He had a peace about him that always intrigued me. He was never too high or too low, even in the midst of competition. This peace that he had went on full display in a moment that I will never forget and which has impacted me more deeply than I ever could have foreseen. He exemplified what "grounded" would come to look like to me.

We were playing the Los Angeles Lakers and I was sitting on the baseline in front of the bench. And we were getting beat pretty good! The late, great Kobe Bryant was schooling our team, and the Lakers were having their way! Kobe was just scoring at will, and we weren't stopping him at all. Needless to say, the environment this created for our team was not great in terms of hope or morale.

But my friend was just being very positive as he was cheering and encouraging the guys on the court. However, there was one other guy on the team who kept turning to him and saying, "Man, how can you cheer for this sh*% ? This sh*% is terrible. This is not worth encouraging. This is just awful bulls@#*. It's all horrible."

But my boy just kept cheering and encouraging our team. Time went by, we were still losing, my friend was still cheering, and the other guy was still hating and being very negative. This went on for maybe fifteen minutes in real time, which is probably a little over half of a quarter (six minutes) in NBA game time.

Finally my friend, without breaking stride, turned to the player that was hating, looked him in the face, and said, "Your attitude is not going to bring me down because Christ is my anchor. You shouldn't let it get you down, either, and if you knew Him you wouldn't be hating like that!" Then he went right back to cheering his team on saying, "Come on, guys, keep going, keep going!" without missing a beat.

I remember just staring at this with my jaw on the ground and marveling at the confidence and poise of my friend. Then the guy who was hating turned and looked right at me! I looked away really fast to make it seem like I hadn't been watching this whole exchange between the two. That was probably one of the most powerful examples of how not to let your environment dictate how you feel about yourself or the situation that I had witnessed in my life up to that point.

I watched this friend often. He would work really hard and do well in practice, but he never got to play one minute in games. Even though it was not easy for him, he just had such a peaceful attitude about being told *no.*How he handled the door constantly being slammed on his dreams really impacted me. I thought, *If I could have that type of peace, I could do a lot more in my life.*

Well, fast forward. My friend ended up retiring, and the team ended up hiring someone who he had worked with in the past when he won a championship with the San Antonio Spurs, as general manager. The new GM approached my friend about coming on board as part of the team's front office staff—offering him a choice between two jobs to continue to be a part of the organization.

The GM told my friend, "I want you to take some time and think about the choices we are offering and make a decision once you take it to the Big Man, because I know that's what you're going to do. And then get back to us and let us know."

He was referring to God as "the Big Man." So my friend prayed about it, took one of the front-office jobs, and is now an assistant coach in the NBA.

One day I asked him, "Why do you think you got the opportunity to do that?"

And my friend told me something really, really profound—simple, but powerful. He said the organization gave him the opportunity to be on their staff because of how he had handled being told "no." They saw his character and how he acted when things didn't go his way. Even when his life was tough, he was still cheering others on and supporting the team. It made the management want to keep him on as part of the organization. They saw he understood the principles of professionalism, which stemmed from the core values he developed. He was grounded in his values about life!

A great starting point to getting grounded is attaching our life values to Someone who is eternal and never changes, and allowing Him to expand them into something greater than we have chosen for ourselves. All our minds are fallible. We have all been wrong about at least one thing, and will be wrong about many more things in the future. This includes ourselves and the value we, and others, might think we have based on our environment.

The Bible says we can be "rooted and grounded in love" (Ephesians 3:17). If we know that we are loved, we come into a place of freedom in who we are, how we're designed, our identity, and our purpose. Our heart gets unlocked, and we see what we are really capable of, what we have the capacity to do, and our capacity for growth.

What I have found thus far on my personal journey is that your past does not dictate your future—unless you let it. If we allow the world to dictate our mindset, it will not give us a sense of being grounded. The world can lead us astray if we allow it to do so. We can be influenced in ways that push us in directions that are unhealthy for our lives and growth as human beings. We also can end up in a place that doesn't bring us peace or fulfillment. When we discover that our lives are filled with purpose, and that purpose is a springboard into destiny, we develop a deeper desire for life. Then we start to discover what our lives are really all about. It opens up fresh new opportunities for us and new doors for others. It also puts us in environments where we get to share our discovery and journey.

Many people tell me they will feel good about themselves when they achieve something. But fame, possessions, status, or the money we accumulate cannot give us grounding, let alone fulfillment. Those things can temporarily give us brief moments of enjoyment, but they are not the foundation to build on for lasting peace. Those temporary moments or experiences can lead us to feel insecure and uncertain about our future. They are not under our control; they are fickle.

There's purpose and destiny for your life! You don't have to conform to the pattern of this world, but you can be transformed into someone greater, more enduring, more stable, and more powerful! Whatever your circumstances may have been in the past, you can be transformed by becoming more established in your mind, dreams, thoughts, and emotions! It is not just something that happens overnight, though; it is an ongoing process—a journey, if you will. But through this process, you can grow into the person you desire to become and to evolve into your greatest self!

CHAPTER
two

{ Lies About
Our Identity }

Understanding our true identity is the biggest step we can take toward feeling grounded in life. Unfortunately, others don't always see or share with us what our true identity is. Sometimes it is up to us to go on the journey to discover it. The greatest hindrances to an empowered identity are the lies we are told to believe about our lives or circumstances.

These lies can be blunt and in-your-face, or they can be very subtle. They can take many forms. They may come from family members, the media, friends, enemies, school, or work. They do not usually appear to be outright lies, or overtly bad, but they take root when we lean on our own understanding, or the world's understanding, to determine what we believe about identity, love, community, and success. Ultimately, every sense of identity we create that does not have a strong grounding in truth will not satisfy us, and can end up ruining us

Importance of Upbringing

The home has an astounding impact on shaping a person's views of their identity as they grow up. If the home is healthy, there is a greater chance that we will become healthy. It's where we get the most communication, the most edification, the most encouragement, the most strengthening, and the most real-life examples of daily living. It's also the place we first start to discover what "trust" looks like to us.

On the flip side, the home could also be the place where we get the most tears, the most neglect, the worst models for communication, and the most discouragement. And it can present the biggest challenges to overcome on the road to understanding our true identity.

Apart from the home, one of the biggest influences on people's views of themselves is the internet. Social media gives us a window into other people's lifestyles, and some people are building their identity through online engagement more than anything else. In the past, we were more likely to be influenced by a group of personal friends in our social circles, our sports teams, etc., but now social media has become more influential than the people we see every day. It also has redefined what being in a relationship with friends looks like, how we engage with one another in community, and how we communicate.

Now, many of us are having our views shaped by what we see on media platforms and streaming services. That content isn't always good, but it is VERY influential. So if someone sees that I'm able to build a following through Instagram, a Facebook live broadast, a TikTok video (or any other social media platform) and see that I've achieved some measure of success in my life, some of them will try to build their identity, resources, and hope by doing the same. They define "success" as being seen by people, having followers, and having an audience that most people wouldn't have access to. Human identity and influence have become the new modern-day currency.

Like money, social media is not good or bad in itself; it is a tool. But if that tool starts to consume your thinking and determine the decisions you make, then it is no longer the tool—you are. Some people are able to find a healthy rhythm and set good boundaries in their lives for that tool; others have completely disengaged from it and don't use social media at all. But sadly, many have allowed it to consume their way of life. That can be very exhausting, especially for those who are trying to discover who they are and what they have been created to do.

But if we are able to root our values well and leverage our ability to connect with others in the right things—by putting our roots in the soil of what God says about us—we are more likely to feel fulfilled and find our purpose in life. When we do that, social media becomes a tool to reach others and help them discover how to do the same. It can empower them to understand that even in our imperfections, we have destiny and purpose. This is social media at its best—when we use it to connect with and edify others, not just empower ourselves.

Right now, even as I'm writing this book, we are dealing with the effects of a global pandemic that has forced most of us to reevaluate how we communicate with one another, how we do family, how we reach one another. It has also forced many to question and reevaluate their identity, because the things that once defined them have been removed or threatened.

We in America are very fortunate to live in a country full of great resources and material wealth. But at times, we try to ground our identity in our house, our car, our technology, our clothes, the media we consume, the school we can afford, etc. Yet I have discovered some of the best understanding about identity comes from spending time with people in other regions where none of those things exist.

I got to travel the world while I was playing professional basketball and through other opportunities afterward. I have seen many people who are destitute, and yet their joy is deep and wide and

their sense of who they are is secure. They do not have the same resources we have here in America, and yet, their environment has not stolen or even impacted their joy. Often, those people have told me they feel like they have enough and that their life is complete. And oh boy, is that usually a shocker to people! Especially those whose identity is in their resources.

I got the opportunity to travel to the Philippines once for some humanitarian service, and went to a place called "Trash Mountain." It was literally the country's dump, and in that dump was an entire community of people. For those born in that dump, the life expectancy is eighteen years because the trash is always burning and the smoke from it is toxic. My heart broke to think that these beautiful people lived in a dump and had no chance of pursuing their dreams, and many would never leave that environment. It crushed me.

I remember walking down the streets and just seeing piles and piles of trash stacked up at least seven stories high. They were literally trash skyscrapers. But entire families still developed a community there. Some of the kids didn't even have clothes, but oddly enough, they still had tremendous joy.

They even had an old basketball hoop in there, so of course I ended up playing with a couple of kids. I will never forget asking one of them, "Why do you have peace?" and "Why are you happy?"

He responded, "It's because we have the presence of God. The presence of God is with us even here in this dump."

Now, that really blew me away that those young kids would have that perspective, despite their environment. To hear their responses was really eye-opening and very humbling, yet really encouraging. It spoke to their truth. In my mind, those kids shouldn't have been joyful—but then I realized that the greatest joy in their lives gave them peace and identity in the midst of their circumstances. They felt they belonged to family, a community, and that gave them hope and security in a very poor, tough, and desolate environment.

What I took away from experiences like that is how we see ourselves and our situation impacts our joy in life tremendously. What we discover about our identity ultimately makes a huge difference in the way we live and how we perceive our situations. Often, we get sidetracked by subtle diversions and lies in our journey through life. However, we don't have to agree with those lies; truth can establish our way and bring us to a greater vision for our lives.

Our Value and Our Life Dreams

We all have to overcome lies about ourselves. I was told many times that I would never go to college. I was told I wasn't smart enough, and that I didn't have the money. I am thankful now I did not believe those lies—and you don't have to believe the lies that were told to you, either!

To overcome lies and walk into our full destiny, we have to be willing to explore what healthy identity looks like for us. Then, we have to be willing to walk out that journey, even if it requires us to be vulnerable in our shortcomings. No, it's not going to be all good; it is going to be very hard and at times, very tiring. But if you know deep in your heart there is something greater for your life, are you willing to try to discover what that is? How much effort are you willing to give to walk into that identity?

I was the first one in my family to go to college and have it fully paid for! I was able to get a college degree, and now my oldest son is the second person in our family ever to go to college. But did the world tell me that was possible? NO! I am living proof that if a dream or vision is in your heart, you can find a way to make it happen, no matter what the world says. Absolutely!

We don't want to make sweeping generalizations about people based on their culture, gender, or family history. We don't want to partner with comments or lies that keep us from being the best version of ourselves. Have you ever heard people say things like, "You're not smart enough"; "You don't have enough resources"; "You're not qualified"; "You don't belong here"; "Women can't do this"; or "Men can't do that"?

A teacher once told me that graduating from high school was as far as I could go, and after that I would work a normal job for the rest of my career. Now, there is nothing wrong with those things— and for some, it is a major accomplishment and their whole dream. However, I believed in my heart I could become a professional basketball player one day. That teacher's words became an obstacle for me to overcome and a lie that was rooted in my thinking.

The one thing that hurt the most about it was that it was coming from someone who had influence on my life, somebody I interacted with every day. She was a person of authority, a person of influence, and a person who had the training to evaluate my academic value. Now, I know that teachers have a lot to juggle, and ultimately, most seek to be positive influences. I have a deep love for educators at every level. Maybe this one thought she was being kind by trying to help me be "realistic," based on her own thoughts. However, when you put a ceiling on a child's dreams while they are still at the incubation stage, it can have a devastating impact on their ability to grow.

Groundedness and Identity

I often heard while I was growing up: "No one in your family has ever amounted to much." One lie that comes from the world that can shape our identity is that we will never be more than our family has been.

When I was younger, a lot of people around me believed what the world said about me: that I was destined to be like many young people growing up without a father, and that I would not amount to much. I felt like I was in a constant battle against that identity others were trying to give me.

Sometimes, our families can get caught up in the same lies the world tries to tell us and can be the ones who unknowingly keep that lie alive and active. My mother experienced these same lies and would sometimes project them onto me without realizing it. She would say, "Greg, you should just grow up and get a job as soon as you can." In her mind, that was the highest standard of achievement—to have a secure job, save up for yourself, save up for your family. She never dreamed of college being an option for herself or me.

One problem with buying into what the world says is that we can put a lid on our own potential. We can give up too soon and not pursue the dreams and goals in our hearts. We can fall short of our best version because we're always being told that things are not going to turn out in our favor, or this is how it's supposed to be because our genealogy or our family history has always been this way.

For example, I know someone who was recruited to go to college on an athletic scholarship. But his family never ventured out of their hometown and basically deterred him from pursuing his dream. His education stopped at high school, which is not a bad thing, but he didn't take advantage of the opportunity to pursue a college education.

It all stemmed from a lie in his family that said, "We never did it, so you can't do it, either." I don't think the family intentionally meant to hurt him; likely they were afraid to lose this person or maybe wanted to protect him from failure. But they didn't encourage him to pursue what could have been a great opportunity.

Our families can impart a sense of groundedness and identity, or a sense of confusion and a series of roadblocks based on their own experiences. Fortunately, my grandmother imparted a sense of groundedness, consistency, and identity to me through what she modeled.

What I saw in my grandmother was steadiness and consistency in some areas of life, as well as the belief in something greater. I remember seeing her pray every day. Quite frankly, I did not like church at all, but I liked seeing her pray. It was a steady constant in her life, a part of her identity that I saw give her strength.

Hearing her pray as she was sitting there every night and early every morning gave me a sense of predictability and comfort. I didn't always know what she was praying, but just seeing her pray consistently impacted me without me even realizing it.

She would always offer to take me to church when she went, but I didn't like going at all. I would listen to the messages there, but I felt uncomfortable; the environment felt rather cold and unwelcoming. I didn't feel good enough to be there or interested enough to stay. While I respected that my grandmother and many others felt differently about it, I didn't feel like I could identify with anything that place had to offer.

Confusion and Roadblocks

In many ways, I grew up longing for what most of us, children and adults alike, long for. We want that sense of belonging. Everybody wants to be at peace. Everyone wants something better for their life. Everyone wants to feel valued. Everyone wants to feel seen, known, and understood. It is good to want that. It drives us to try to find it. But sometimes it can drive us in the wrong direction, if there are not good people in our lives pointing the way or we don't have healthy boundaries. It can potentially set us back many years en route to achieving our dreams and goals.

My mom, at times was not my biggest advocate in trying to achieve my dreams. She tried her best to help me get along in life, yet her limitations weren't the dream I had for myself. Nonetheless, in her love and own way, she did model some amazing things to me that ended up really shaping my understanding of certain areas of my life. She taught me about community and hard work. (I will share more on this later.)

But she also believed some lies that I inherited. These created a false sense of identity for me. If we are not grounded, when others speak a false identity over us, it can tear us down, distract us, and even knock us off course in life.

When I started playing professional basketball, I was playing overseas. Once, while I was between jobs and waiting on another opportunity, I called my mom for encouragement. She told me, "It's just best that you stay home, become a regular working person, and accept that you're not going to be able to play anymore." That broke my heart because, at the time, I was really hoping for emotional support for my hopes, dreams, and identity.

But I wasn't getting that from her. Also, I realized later I was putting pressure on her to give it to me because I was struggling to be assured within myself. I know now that was not really fair. She could only encourage me in what she had seen working in her own life, which was trying to find a steady job (of any kind) and focusing on building happiness around times with family.

Hearing her say that put me in a very bad space. Not only relationally with her, but with myself. Looking back on it, I can see that I was putting a lot of my faith in what my mom was thinking and what she said to me, instead of in something that was true about me. Her words did not bring me life. Ultimately, I think we damage a lot of relationships and suffer a lot of disappointment when we fail to realize that other people cannot do what God is meant to do—which is to give us an unshakable identity and reassure us of our calling in the way we need when we need it.

Another way my home life negatively impacted me while I was young was that my mom lived a promiscuous lifestyle. Generations of my family had been born from sex without commitment and love, and she followed in those footsteps. For a time, I thought this was part of my identity. I was born from this way of living, and I started to live that way myself.

The breaking point for me came when I was an adult. One night, after I slept with a woman, she rolled over and said, "Hey, can you tell me that you love me?" And at that point, I just flat-out told her, "I don't even love myself."

I felt like I wasn't in control of myself. Like I was a slave anytime that urge came on me. I felt very helpless, I felt very broken, and I felt as if I had no morals in my life. In that moment, my heart was devastated; it felt as if someone had turned off all the color in my life. Although the world would say that was supposed to be a moment of pleasure, it turned out to be one of the most shattering moments of my life.

I knew at some point I would want to marry a woman and actually have a family. I didn't want to be the guy who cheats on his wife. I saw all the pain and destruction that comes from that and how it impacted me as a kid—how it impacts generations, your whole family line. It impacts your opportunities, your finances, your reputation, and physiological understanding of what love is. It's a very destructive mindset to inherit.

I began to have an affection for women early on because that's who I grew up around. The women in my life did their best to answer my questions and fill in gaps where I was struggling from not having a male influence.

But not having a father figure in the house still impacted me greatly. I felt like I was often simply in "survival mode." I grappled with many feelings of bitterness, pain, and neglect because of this vacancy in my life. So I developed a defense mechanism to try to distract myself from those feelings. At a young age, I vowed that if I ever had children, I would try to be there for them as much as I could as a father. So I spent time thinking about what I thought a dad should be like—what he would do and how he would act.

As various male figures drifted through my life, I gravitated toward the ones that represented some type of good to me. I'd compile what I thought my dad would look like in my heart based on them. So if my mom brought a man around the house who was kind, I would take that small act of kindness and tuck it away in my heart. Then, I would meet another man who was passionate, another who was driven, another who spoke well, another who had a taste for culture or music. I would just take all the good characteristics out of all the men I met and compile them in my heart. I was always looking for what I felt was missing in my life and in myself.

I thought my dad would have all the best attributes of all the male figures I met over the course of my upbringing. Now, some of them did *not* model good things, and some of the things I thought were good at the time ended up not being so good. But what I took away from all that was the feeling that there must be something greater than me, and I wanted to be a part of it! There must be something "out there" that would cause me to feel I had roots, stability, hope for my future, and strength to continue in hard times. I wanted to know I was surrounded by support, love, acceptance, and hope.

A Grounded Identity Formed by the Truth, the Life, and the Way
There are many ways that having an identity grounded in truth is helpful. We need to believe there's hope for us. There's hope for our lives. There's hope for our futures. There's hope even in our failures. We need to believe there's promise and freedom for our lives.

So, how do we do this? First, we need to believe a truth about us that is based on something bigger than anyone's thoughts, including our own! Truth manifests by the fruit coming out of our lives. The question we should ask is, "What is my life producing? Is it love, positivity, hope, and joy? Connections with people who encourage and genuinely help me feel more confident about myself? Am I living according to a truth that is causing me to become a better person, someone I can be proud of? A person who inspires society?"

Maybe you think you are just naturally a good person, but I would ask: Are you motivated by self-centered goals, or goals centered on others? Because when our goals are self-centered, they don't have the power to last. However, when they are centered on others, they can impact society on a greater scale. They also end up fulfilling our own dreams along the way.

The problem with leaning on our own understanding for our identity is that we are all human and fallible. Sometimes, we abandon the truth about ourselves and let our circumstances, family, history of failure, or the world start to tell us who we are. It's extremely difficult to have long-term success if we rely on unstable, short-term things to give us identity. However, we become grounded when we attach our view of life to Someone bigger than we are, Someone who is eternal and never changes.

Truth should bring us life and passion for others. What do I mean by "life"? I am referring to that feeling of hope, freedom, and purpose. These attributes bring life to others around us. The biggest catalyst for growth and freedom is having a sense that you are living according to what you see in a hopeful future, not what someone else sees and determines for your life. There is opportunity for our lives if we are able to let go of the limits the world puts on us.

I am not talking about the short-lived emotional high of pursuing material things or the approval of people. That can let us down, especially if we base our identity on those things. But pursuing a greater purpose that is focused on helping others and making a positive difference will not let you down. It actually gives you life and a greater reason to make a difference.

Finding life is also not about just doing what feels good in the moment. It is more sustainable than just one moment or a collection of moments. It takes into account what brings life to others. If something makes me feel good but hurts others, that may take me off my path and ultimately bring more feelings of destruction in my heart. That indicates I need to reassess my goals.

The Bible tells us to live according to "the way." What is the way? It is knowing your purpose and what drives you in life. This is a powerful way to overcome challenges. This helps us make decisions. When we go through seasons and difficult circumstances, we gain steadiness from knowing we are living according to a greater purpose.

We get grounded by seeing we are always on the way to a greater journey. Many of us in the United States are taught by our culture that we should be goal-oriented—focused on outcomes and accomplishments. I'm not saying we shouldn't have goals or things we want to achieve in our lives. However, we tend to be happier and more fulfilled when we focus on accomplishing these goals through partnership with others. It feels amazing to develop relationships with people as you work together toward a common purpose.

When we are grounded in the truth, the life, and the way, we start to feel we have an inner compass. I didn't feel I had a compass at all early on. But now, I can't imagine going through life without it! This compass not only directs us toward success but helps us to get back on track when we get distracted. Only with a sense of identity can we lean into our mistakes, lean into our doubts, lean into the places that we fall short, and still stand. We can move past our failures and the lies we've heard toward victory.

When we are authentic, we are available, present, and an example of hope to others. You can be flawed and still have so much promise for your life. I am living proof of that!

Finally, when we become grounded in our identity, we start to naturally desire to give back to our community and the people around us. People can identify with our journey, and that gives us the power to impact our community when we share our stories. That gives those around us a chance to see what is possible for them, too. They will see that we have hope, peace, joy, and that we're willing to learn, we're willing to grow, we're willing to take feedback, we're willing to even take criticism and not be offended because our identity is not in pleasing people. Its in your desire to become a better person.

Even if you don't play sports or do anything highly visible, you can add value to your community. You can be the person who speaks identity into others' lives and powerfully impacts them forever. You add value by telling them the truth about them instead of lies, that the world may be trying to dictate to them. You can simply be an encouragement to others; that alone is a lost art in our society.

True success is the ability to find the good in everything you go through. That includes the hard stuff, the trying times, the seasons when we are tired and exhausted. When we know our ultimate identity and where we gain strength, compassion, and hope, we never have to depend on anyone else to understand us or say the right words to us.

The potential for your life is as vast as the ocean. You can't even see the end of it! Your sight only allows you to see to a certain distance, but God sees it all and He has so much in store for you—more than what you can see or imagine. There's so much promise for our lives when He's in the center of them. That is why having an identity that is grounded in Him is the most successful and impactful sense of identity we can have.

Sounds great, huh? But how do we get there? How did I get from living off the opinions of others to living connected to the way, the truth, and the life and all the benefits that come from that?

Well, what happened next you might not want to know. My family didn't even want to know! (Truth be told, I didn't even want to know, haha.) I had a lot of assumptions at the time. But what I went through got me free. I had to set aside all my preconceived ideas, and be willing to pursue the way, the truth, and the life no matter what.

And that is what I would ask from you as well. If you really want a better life and believe you deserve to live from victory, I am here to tell you that you do! It will not always be easy, but it will always be worth it. The question is, how much do you actually want it? If you don't want it, it might be best to close this book now. But if even a small part of you wants something greater, then keep reading.

CHAPTER
three

{ The Midnight
Meeting }

Until I learned what it meant to be grounded and have a strong identity, I spent a lot of time trying to make people care about and be happy with me. It didn't matter who they were, I thought i f I could convince them that I was not the stereotypical guy my age with my background, then I would finally be OK in life. I tried to fit in on the bus in elementary school by making mean jokes about people; I tried to fit in on sports teams by being the best. I tried all these different ways to get others to embrace me. Quite frankly, none of it seemed to work, and more often than not, I had to deal with their rejection.

I used to constantly strive to make everyone around me happy, and I found it to be more exhausting than fulfilling. Maybe you can relate? The prettiest girl in my high school was one of the only African American girls there. I would often tell myself, "This girl is way out of my league," but I would always catch her looking at me with a smile. My friends would say, "She's beautiful, but she's a holy girl. You can't talk to her." I was petrified because I felt that if I talked to her, I would have to become holy like her, a good person. Deep down, I felt that I had to change and honestly, I was ashamed of the person I was hiding behind my facade. I automatically disqualified myself from talking to that girl, because deep down I had yet to discover any true value in myself.

This young girl was a Christian, and that was a problem (or so I thought)! As I stated earlier, I did not go to church. I wanted to hang out with her, but I knew that in order to make her happy or even have a chance to get her to go out with me, I would have to go to her church. Well, sure enough, I did! Nevertheless, my bout with being a holy boy did not last long because I could not shake the feeling of not belonging and not being good enough. Inside, I felt I could not level up enough to feel like I was worthy of this relationship. I thought so little of myself at the time that there was no way I could be with someone so pure. I also had no male guidance on how to approach a girl I actually liked without completely sabotaging the whole thing before even taking one step.

The familiar feeling of not being good enough came up again years later, when I was playing professional basketball. One of my coaches and I really hit it off and became friends. One night, I stayed at his house with his family. We all got into a deep discussion about God and our experiences with church. My coach had a profound affection for God and talked about Him in really intriguing ways. At the time, I did not recognize that God was impacting my life in any way.

I would talk to my coach about God, but I didn't have any sense of identity, groundedness, or power to keep me from feeling like a victim in life. None of my accomplishments were big enough. Not college, not professional sports. I still felt I had to always prove myself.

I kept losing my cool, cussing up a storm when things went bad, going out and sleeping with girls. Meanwhile, I was acting all Christian with that coach. I was trying to perform in the ways I thought I had to in order to make everyone happy and accept me all the time. I didn't realize that I needed to first accept myself.

How was I going to learn to do that? I didn't like a lot of things about myself: I didn't have a father; I didn't have the greatest opportunities handed to me; I didn't feel people believed in me, or thought I was good enough for them. I often heard people say I wouldn't amount to much. I battled thoughts of suicide as a young kid. Looking back, I would say my mental health was not as strong as I was portraying it to be on the outside. I faked confidence by watching others around me, but I was never fulfilled within myself. It was a very confusing, fatiguing way to go through life as a young man.

I had a lot of reservations about faith. I thought it meant that you had to be perfect, or at least try to be. I wasn't perfect by any means (and I am still not). And I knew I could not uphold the reputation of being perfect. It was just too much pressure.

I thought God was Someone who was way off somewhere. I think I saw Him the way I did my own father: someone who didn't know me. I thought I had to do good things or be incredibly successful or famous for Him to care about me. I thought I would not be able to be myself around Him, and would have to perform and be successful in life to make Him proud.

But all that changed, literally overnight. It's hard to explain, but I had an experience that put me on a trajectory from being lost, confused, and feeling like a hopeless victim to experiencing some of the greatest victories of my life and discovering my true identity.

The Late-Night Meeting

Upon this journey I got a chance to discover that grace and truth always flow to the lowest places—and the biggest change in my life took place when I was in the lowest space. I had just gotten fired from my basketball job. I was cut from my team and sent home. This crushed me. It was what I was hinging my identity on at the time—my ability to perform in basketball. I felt like I had nothing left, so I was really heading into a tailspin. I had just come back from a major surgery on my knee, I had overcome being out of playing professionally for a year, and my girlfriend and I had just had our **second** child. There was a lot more riding on my success this time around. But it all came crashing down when I was told no and sent home from my opportunity overseas.

However, two miraculous things happened while I was in that tailspin: The first was that my old job as **an overnight security guard** in the small town where I was living had laid off a lot of people—and even though I hadn't even been there for a while, they didn't lay me off. I was able to come back from overseas and go right back to work. That kept me going a little, to know I had something. The second miracle was that at work one night, I spoke to a friend who was at a point in his life studying to become a pastor. I called him because he worked the night shift like I did.

We talked about God and his experience with faith. At the end of our conversation, he simply suggested that I should check out a church in San Diego. He said I would like the pastor because he's funny and he played sports. Well, I love comedy and I play sports, so I thought, *What do I have to lose?* He said to go online and watch the services. I went online and watched about three messages.

At the end of his third message, the pastor offered an invitation to receive God and start a relationship with Him. That's when the strangest thing happened. I remember the room I was sitting in just getting really warm and really bright. And I was like, *Man, am I having a panic attack?* Am I having a heart attack? It kinda freaked me out, but it didn't feel like there was a threat. I just knew that something was happening. On the video, the pastor said, "If you want to receive God, I want you to lift your hands wherever you are."

I remember raising my hands and thinking that I was ready to make a real commitment. I remember saying, "Here I am, I give You all my life. All my living days, I'm going to be walking with You." And I had no idea what I was doing or why, but I just started weeping and crying profusely. It felt like a good hour that I spent just crying.

I tried to compose myself, but this overwhelming feeling of acceptance, compassion, and peace consumed the room, my body and mind. Finally the room shifted back to my regular work scene and was completely normal again. When I went home, I told my girlfriend (now my wife), who I was living with at the time, what had happened. I told her that I had accepted Jesus Christ as my Lord and Savior. She didn't know what that meant. She was like, "Well, what does that mean?" And I said, "Man, I'm not sure, I'm just going to follow God all my living days."

I felt like I had discovered the starting point toward my purpose. I felt I had found my way, even though I didn't totally understand what it all meant at that point. I told my now-wife that I needed to get on a plane and fly to San Diego (where I had grown up) to meet the pastor whose sermon I had watched. She thought I was just going through a weird time. She didn't get it and neither did I. Yet, I had to do what was strongly being impressed upon my heart. About a month later, I flew from my home in Washington state down to my former home in San Diego.

As I was leaving, I called a few of my old friends. The one who had suggested I watch the sermon online was the first person I called to share my news with. I thought he would think this was great! I said, "Hey, man I'm flying back home, I would like to go to the church you suggested I watch online. Would you go with me? Let's get up in the front row. I'm going to meet the pastor."

Well, he started laughing at me like, "What do you mean?" This church was a big church. He was like, "Did the pastor call and say he would meet with you? Are you sure the pastor you're looking for is even going to be there?" I said, "No. I just feel like this is my way forward, that God wants me to get on a plane and go meet him."

And then my friend really started laughing at me. He said, "Man, it doesn't work that way, man! You can't just show up and go see the pastor."

And I was like, "I don't know. I feel like I'm being told to go meet this man. I already bought my plane ticket."

He said, "All right, fine, I'll go with you, but don't get your hopes up."

So, Sunday arrived, and we ended up going down to the church. The pastor was actually there, too! He came out and preached, and when the service was over he stood at the side of the stage. There was a sea of people in front of him. I'm not gonna lie, I was a bit frustrated and actually was about to grab my friend and just leave. But I felt confident that I was supposed to say something.

I said in my head, *Man, God, here I am. I feel like I was supposed to come here, that You brought me here, so make it happen.* I turned my back to the pastor and people, then turned back around and the pastor was there looking at me with his arms folded. So I walked right up to him, introduced myself and then to my surprise, heard myself say, "I believe God wants me to go into ministry."

To be honest, I didn't even know what that word, "ministry," meant, but it seemed right. The pastor started joking with me like, "Man, how old are you, young blood?" I told him my age. And he was like, "Man, I'm about to be fifty. Can you believe that, man? But I still look good, though. You know it!!" And he was just joking with me and fixing my collar on my jacket.

I said, "I felt like God told me to come down here and for you to pray for me." So he put his hands on my shoulders. I put my hands on his shoulders, and the first thing that shot through my mind was that this was a monumental moment in my life. God spoke to me: *Now it is happening.* And I thought, *I wish I had a picture of this amazing moment.*

The pastor finished praying and we agreed to stay in touch. Then, as I was walking away, a girl walked up to me and said, "Hey, the *LA Times* is writing a front-page article on the church and they want to know if they can use this picture?"

She flipped her camera around to show me a picture of me and the pastor with our heads bowed, our hands on each other's shoulders, praying. And I thought to myself, *WOW, God, does it work that fast? I didn't even say anything.* And I was thinking to myself, *Man, if He made a prayer and a picture happen like that, what is He going to do with the rest of my life?* I actually still have that picture. It was on the front page of the *LA Times*. It felt like suddenly I had found a way, real life, and I was starting to seek more of the truth.

My views on God started to change immediately. I finally got to actually know Him as He is, not just my own assumptions and ideas about Him. Not my grandmother's ideas, or my coach's ideas. He really started to rebuild my foundation of who He is. One of the biggest changes, I realized, was that with God, I did not have to earn the blessings or try to portray myself as somebody I really wasn't. In

the hardest part of my life, He made a way for me to keep my job, to watch that sermon, to meet the senior pastor, and even to be with him in a picture on the front page of the *Los Angeles Times*. I didn't earn or deserve any of those blessings. It was just a gift of grace given to me freely.

Right out of the gate, it contradicted the feeling that I needed to do things in order to be accepted or loved by God; I was just saved and forgiven by His grace. All I had to do was trust. Trust was the entry point for blessing and the starting point for a new journey.

Now, let's check in for a minute. I know it might not make total sense, and you might have a lot of questions and feel skeptical about the things I just wrote. But I want to share a glimpse of something better with you. The greatest thing is that you don't have to fully agree or understand to stay on this journey toward greater things with me, just as my friend had with me before I got on board.

Often, our greatest opportunities are birthed out of our willingness to explore things we don't understand. I didn't understand what it meant to walk with God; however, I was willing to see what that looked like. That led me to watch an online church service that changed my life forever. For you, that willingness may be continuing to read this book with me, even though you may have some reservations. That is normal and OK, and you are welcome here!

I want to encourage any of you who may not feel ready to take a leap of faith that comprehension is not a prerequisite for cooperation. You don't have to understand or fully be convinced of God to cooperate with this information. For some of you, this may be an opportunity just to gain principles to help you move forward in life.

I want to say that again: your comprehension is not a prerequisite for your cooperation. So you don't have to fully feel you understand anything at this moment. Simply showing up and considering these things is what starts to qualify you. It starts to make more sense as you continue to explore with an open heart and open mind.

Actions Speak Louder than Words

Committing my life to God was only the first step in my journey to fully uncovering the way, the truth, and the life that was in store for me. There was and is so much more. I realized I had been seeing glimpses of what I wanted in life from people I met or things I experienced. But I realized those things I admired were mostly things that came from GOD. When I feel like I fall flat on my face, He's still there cheering me on. I saw that in my friend the basketball player—even when it looked like the other team was winning, he was supporting his team. He never let the situations change his feelings and support.

That whole concept changed my idea of who God is. Especially who He is as a father. He was not condemning me, ignoring me, waiting for me to be better, or "earn" His attention.

As I write this book we are dealing with a global pandemic. However, I'd like to suggest an even greater pandemic in our societies is all the young children growing up in fatherless homes. Others have fathers who are physically present but not emotionally or mentally engaged with their homes or children. Often, these young children lose their way at a young age. In the Gospel of John, someone asks Jesus, "How can we know the way?" and Jesus answers, "I am the way and the truth and the life. No one comes to the Father except through Me." This revelation (new understanding) really hit me. I had always wanted to be able to go to a father to get an idea of what real life was. When I read that verse, it was like Jesus was speaking directly to me.

From having my own son now, and working with a lot of young people, I can say it's very important to know your dad is championing you. That your dad is there for you, that your dad accepts you just the same whether you "succeed" or "fail." That no matter what you do, he's there for you and with you, and he'll walk with you as you're growing. I knew I didn't have that growing up, and yet, now, because of God, I no longer had to live as a victim of my parents' decisions or other people's opinions.

I felt so free. I could fall, stand up, dust myself off, and continually press forward. I could connect with God not only based on my triumphs, but my failures and God's victory despite them.

The Beginning of Victory through Sacrifice

I soon realized that the Bible was not a list of rules, but actually a guidebook and love story to help me live life free from the lies that had been spoken about me and the things that had been done to me. It even let me live free from my own thoughts, judgments, and failures! That is incredible! As I started to see more of God, I saw more of who I could be as His son.

There were some immediate changes after my bizarre encounter with God. But the people around me did not always receive them well. For the first time, I had to learn how to not make my decisions based on others' opinions, but on the inner compass I had found— the way, the truth, and the life inside me. The first thing this impacted in my life was my speech.

Before that encounter, I had cussed a lot. I was hot-tempered; I would fly off the handle and lose my cool. Even to this day, God is still constantly picking me up when I fail and helping me to keep working on these areas in my life.

Another immediate change I made was to stop listening to certain kinds of music and watching certain movies and TV shows. Music that made me feel angry, that made me feel like objectifying women, or that filled my mind with things that did not bring life to me or others went out the door. Although I was raised on that stuff, it just wasn't good for me. I am not saying the people who make or listen to that music are bad, but the message was not healthy by any means for me as a maturing adult. It was not the truth I wanted for myself, and it was poisoning my mind and my heart.

As I mentioned, my family and friends did not always support my decision because it meant I had to extract myself from some circles or patterns of behavior they were used to. I stopped smoking weed, drinking, hanging out, sleeping around, etc. I didn't do that anymore.

But this behavior change wasn't because I was trying to be holy or perfect. I was just trying to keep a sense of the way, the truth, and the life growing inside me, and I found those things were getting in the way. I knew there was a journey I had to go on, and this was a part of the journey I needed to relinquish in order to really absorb and inherit the Kingdom of God and what that would look like as a lifestyle.

Sometimes, it was very painful because I felt like all these things were being taken away from me. I didn't want them to be, but I finally realized some of the people in my life were not the kind of people I really admired; they were just people who I wanted to accept me. All these relationships were being lost because my values started to change.

But it felt like the foundation that had been unstable since my childhood was finally being healed. The wounds from not having a father. Things I had seen and had been invited into and things that made me feel "less than." Things that were missing in my growth and maturity as a man, father, and a person of faith. As I changed, I found myself developing a beautiful new community of people who helped shape my views for the better.

This was the turning point in my life. And what I realized was that a journey to know the way, the truth, and life did require sacrifice. Like any great story, sacrifice was the way out of being a victim and the starting point into a place of victory.

The first thing I had to sacrifice were my old thoughts about God and who He was. None of us likes being misunderstood. None of us likes being misjudged on negative things others say about us. None of us likes being lied about. But get this: God has been more misunderstood, misjudged, and lied about than any of us. And I was an offender.

I had projected my experiences with people I knew onto Him. In other words, I thought He was more like what people said about Him than what He said about Himself. I also believed that He was a God who rewarded good behavior and punished bad. I thought I had to do things to be rewarded, as if it was some kind of formula. My perception of God was so backward that it exhausted me more than encouraged me.

Most of the Christians I know start out their faith journey this same way. We have to be careful at the beginning not to mix up who God is with who people are. We can't accept their opinions and descriptions without being willing to discover who He is for ourselves. Otherwise, we will be misled and disappointed. My idea of God stemmed from always desiring attention because of the void in my life from my father. I really battled with this when I was younger. Even into my adult years, it took me a while to identify the root of my outbursts, bouts of depression, anxiety, etc. I discovered it was all rooted in my desire for acceptance.

One thing that has always meant a lot to me is encouragement (affirmation). That was always something I craved. Even just hearing, "You're doing good. You're going the right way." I never got that when I was young. I certainly didn't get it without earning it. But God is different; He affirms based on His sovereignty and grace and our being renewed in His Son, not on how we perform or what we do.

I also had to sacrifice a belief that God's forgiveness didn't apply to me. I had a really hard time with that. I had this idea of having to walk in perfection, yet there were things in my life I was really ashamed of—things that came out of my mouth, my lifestyle, what I was doing, being sneaky, lying, exaggerating, etc. It felt like my life was hollow and not fulfilling. I would have moments of joy, yet it wasn't a genuine joy. It was a made-up impression of it.

I didn't feel like God was going to forgive me for those things. I felt like every time I did something bad, He was going to hold it over my head and I was going to have to pay the price. I didn't see there was grace for when I acted poorly, that God's grace could cover it. I *would* have to walk out the consequences of my mistakes; however, I didn't know I could have Someone walk with me and heal me of my past at the same time.

I guess I was trying to treat Him like a human in some ways, not realizing how different He was from humans who had hurt me or misrepresented Him to me. Instead, He was Someone who accepted me unconditionally. This was so unfamiliar to me. My reality was to embrace what was toxic, and I did not have the ability to see or embrace what was healthy. It was a very lonely space emotionally, mentally, and spiritually.

Have you ever felt this way?

Yet, the more time I spent with Him, the more I could hear what I needed from Him. I realized more about the truth of who I actually was and my identity. I was unconditionally loved; I didn't have to be perfect; I was already worthy. This helped me start to combat all the lies that had been spoken over me. Finally, I was connected to Someone bigger than me, who was not just another human with an opinion but who Himself was everlasting life. His Truth about me was truer than mine was! It was the most liberating revelation I have ever received.

When you're surrendered to God, you can know the truth about yourself. You're also able to see the good that comes from this as you start to reflect good things to other people, just like most people grow up reflecting the people around them in their environment. I started to become aware of being a reflection of His love, being a reflection of His grace and His redemptive power for each situation. My idea of faith, love, and life had been shaped by unhealthy rejection. Yet when God stepped into the picture, His life of redemption started to help me come to a place of healthy reflection.

When I really gave my life to Jesus and started following Him, it started to repair and rebuild the foundation of my life. My first couple of years, it was just learning by trial and error. I was on an expedited learning track and it gave me some opportunities to make mistakes. But then I got to see what grace looked like and what a healthy environment looked like where I could mess up but get back up.

Not only did I meet God, I met my way, truth, and life—and you can, too. This meeting changed the entire course of my life. I went from getting fired from professional basketball, to going back to a regular job, to going to San Diego, to the wildest adventure of my life.

Soon, I would be going into different parts of the world—even anti-Christian and very hostile places—and sharing what I had found out about God, not just in words, but by loving those communities through my actions.

CHAPTER
four

{ Overcoming
Rejection }

When I was in eighth grade, I asked my basketball coach for a ride home from the gym.

He told me, "I'm not going that way, you need to walk home."

At first, I didn't think anything of it. I made the long trek home. But when I was a block away from my house, I saw him drive by with a bunch of other kids in his car—the same kids from my team I had just been practicing with! He didn't stop, beep his horn, or anything. He just rolled past me.

I later asked him why I couldn't have a ride, too, and he said it was because I wasn't a good enough player. Ouch!

I felt so rejected in that moment. Not only did his words lead me to believe I wasn't good enough at my sport, but they planted something in me that said I wasn't worthy, period. They started to create a narrative in my mind that I was rejected at my core and I always would be. That moment turned into a root of rejection that started to shape my feelings of not being worthy of anything, including love from others. From that point forward, I was always fighting to prove that I was.

I was already feeling rejected because my dad wasn't around; I believed it was because I wasn't worth his spending time with me. I thought that was why he'd never taken the time to reach out and meet me. My coach's comment not only reinforced that idea, but said moreover, I wasn't valued by other people, either. I started to collect all the reasons I wasn't worthy of love. I believed that if I became successful or did something others approved of, I could prove them wrong, have power over them. But, wow, was I wrong!

Little did I know, I was creating a foundation for my life that was completely unstable and would bring me nothing but harm. I didn't know better at the time, and I don't think it was wrong of me to feel that way. It wasn't wrong to say I was rejected—that was true, especially compared to all those other kids that day. Yet the rejections *in* our lives shouldn't become the projections *for* our lives.

But as we will discuss in the next chapter, rejection was not the highest truth about me. It was a human's truth about me, but it was not God's truth about me. Yet I took others' actions and words seriously back then because I didn't know there was a higher truth about me. I accepted their truths unquestioningly, and then started to wear them like ragged clothes. They didn't fit me, even though I was wearing them. Human truths will always fail us and cause us to feel unstable unless they are built on love. And I did not see a lot of truth about myself based on love coming from the people around me. I was buying into their misguided truths, but that was like embracing a ticking time bomb: it will never bring a good result. It was slowly eroding my confidence and identity.

That narrative almost debilitated me.

When you are developing a sense of identity, any type of rejection can be a great detriment to your growth. It can take you off your path to your destiny. Maybe you can think right now of some moments when you were rejected and how it made you feel! If we do not feel a sense of acceptance from family and community, we tend to start looking for love in other areas that are synthetic or fake, such as social media "likes," making money, fitting in, or even joining gangs or other groups of people who give us a momentary feeling of acceptance.

We are wired to desire love—and we will accept it even when it is not good for us or comes from people holding their own ticking time bombs. We feel that is all we are worth. We feel like we belong with them because our narratives match, but later we find ourselves casualties of all the explosions going on around us. Those connections only bring more pain into our lives.

We start to search for fulfillment in our hearts after feeling rejected in our homes, schools, and workplaces. Rejection can lead to a root of bitterness and start to challenge our true identities as human beings. It makes us lesser versions of ourselves, it makes us expect less for ourselves, and as a result we pursue less of what our real selves have to offer.

We're most impressionable when we're young, and that is when these seeds get planted in our hearts. We are like a field at the mercy of what is planted; as people plant love and acceptance or hate and rejection, we see those things grow.

From a young age, we are conscious enough to be be aware of some sense of identity. That stage of life is so critical. You can be told some really profound and powerful things that can put you on a trajectory for greatness and destiny, or you can be told lies that put you on a trajectory for self-destruction.

We also inherit seeds planted in our family line. If they are seeds of bitterness, anger, rejection, and isolation, they will grow into barriers and walls in our lives. We can become grounded in anger and rejection instead of love. But the fruit produced by anger and rejection is bitter poison and not something that brings life to us or the people around us. This happened to me. If my life was a field, rejection was its best crop! It was thriving like a weed, sucking the life and nutrients from the soil, producing things that no one really valued or seemed to enjoy—and that only made me feel worse.

That was, until I discovered a greater truth and way of peace by giving my life to God. I am not going to lie: it was hard at times. It required a lot of uprooting and digging in areas that didn't feel so good to revisit or even identify. As I allowed Him greater access to my heart, He was like a gardener who started to uproot the things that were poisoning me. It was the most sobering, gut-wrenching time in my life. However it was also the most necessary.

At times, I felt I had a right to keep those things, and I wanted to hold onto them. But then I started to ask why I was so committed to holding onto the opinions, judgments, and rejection that were actively hurting me?

Now, that is not to say I was never rejected again in any way after I let God in. Not at all! But how I handle it is different now that my foundation is strong. I now know a greater truth that makes me feel accepted even in the midst of rejection, and that keeps me from growing more poisonous fruit.

This was a big battle, but one that I am relieved and happy to know I have made some big strides in. I want to share that victory with you. In this chapter, I want to talk about what makes us vulnerable to rejection, how to identify the root when we're feeling rejected, and then share three practical antidotes to it. The good news is, we can all be grounded in our identity and in peace and contentment—even when we have less-than-ideal experiences or circumstances in life. Let's take a look.

What Makes Us Vulnerable to a Spirit of Rejection

For those of us who have struggled with rejection at the core of our identity, survival was more important than dreaming when we were growing up. It is hard to reflect or grow when you're in survival mode. When I was growing up, my mom was really focused on providing for us. We didn't have a chance to have long talks, and I didn't get to ask the kinds of profound questions that could shape my identity when I was young.

Don't get me wrong—single parents are absolutely amazing! They are usually trying their best in a situation that most of the time, they never wanted or asked for. They have often experienced significant pain as well, and work extremely hard to ensure their family survives. But it is rare for a child to have a strong sense of being cared for and tended to when a parent doesn't have that sense themselves.

Sometimes, kids from single-parent homes are fortunate enough to have help from a family member or someone in the community, and that goes a long way in helping the whole family. It serves as a buffer to keep seeds of rejection from taking root, and also helps to establish some type of healthy understanding of what care looks like.

Yet even when there are two parents in the home, there is not always time, space, or understanding of how to care. Rejection can develop then, too. Sometimes, rejection can develop from an accumulation of circumstances like the ones I had, where a coach or a teacher (or both) do not place value on you as a person.

It can also happen if you were ostracized by friends, teased, bullied, or ignored by your peers. This form of neglect is part of "cancel culture"—which, at its root, causes a person to feel they are no longer accepted because they don't hold the "right" ideas. It could happen if you do not get picked for a team, a school, a scholarship, or any number of things. It could happen if you feel like something makes you different from others in a bad way. This could be anything from physical ability to race, gender, hair color, you name it. You can feel rejected by organizations—even churches. You can feel like you are invisible—or worse, canceled. But take heart: there is hope.

The good news is that there are things that can counterbalance moments of rejection, ways to uproot those poisonous plants and create space to nurture life-giving ones. There is hope for all of us who find ourselves at this place in life.

Signs of Rejection
Sometimes we don't even realize we are living in rejection, so it helps to know some of the signs of rejection that might show up in our lives. Often, these will play out throughout one's life. For instance, you might become a recluse, becoming quiet and withdrawn. Or you might start doing things just to be noticed—for some ladies, it's getting noticed because of your body; for guys, it may be athletic ability or having multiple sex partners. Others

might start to idolize making money and success over how they treat people.

All these responses are common reactions to rejection. A lot of times, we find people who are lonely, broken, and sad who are trying to cover those things up instead of looking for ways to be empowered and more fulfilled.

Because I didn't grow up knowing what healthy love looked like or what it meant to be in love with someone, sex became the weapon I used to fight rejection, something that gave me a false sense of accomplishment. It was a way to gain status and meet my needs. I had to learn later how to express love sexually through intimacy with my wife. What I had thought was "love" were really behaviors that I was using to try to hide my own sense of rejection, and by resorting to them I was setting myself up to feel more rejected and unloved than before.

A seed was planted in my heart early on concerning love and women. As I got older, that seed grew into a weed that started to shape my perspective on the issue. Before long, I was robbed of a healthy, connecting, meaningful, and fulfilling view of sex and intimacy. When you don't see examples of people living free of rejection as a young person, you see how people around you act and start to think that is normal, even healthy.

Entire groups of people can feel connected by their mutual feelings of rejection. And when that happens, we do not always realize how it steals away our identity and healthy understanding of things like love, sex, and family. We do not know that a healthy understanding of them will bring us feelings of acceptance, connection, and peace.

Jesus Experienced Rejection
Now that I am a Christian, every time I start to question what I can or can't do based on my family background, what someone says about me, or how they treat me, I think of Jesus. I know you might

be thinking, "How could Jesus know anything about rejection when He was God's Son?" Well, let's just say that I rejected Him for a long time, as many others have and still do. Sadly, He has had more people reject Him than any of us have ever had!

Get this: Many people believed Jesus was an illegitimate child, which was a big problem in His culture. He was not born to a rich or special family. He was literally born in an animal stable to a poor carpenter and his teenage wife because they had nowhere else to go when He was born.

As He grew up, even the people close to Him doubted Him and His destiny and calling. In Mark 6, when Jesus started to teach, people asked, "Is this not the carpenter, the son of Mary?" Back then, teaching was reserved for people of higher status, so His own people basically said He was not going to be a teacher—He was just a lowly carpenter. They set their limitations on Him and rejected Him.

On top of that, His whole family line could have set Him up to feel rejected and alone. In those days, lineage was of highest importance. Pure lines were valued—that is, people who had only ever married good, observant Jews were seen as more valuable and respectable. So what was Jesus's family line like? Among his lineage were a prostitute, a murderer, a liar, and a deceiver. People the world would say were not good enough, or inferior in some way. They could easily have said, "Hey, you're going to be these things, too; this is where you come from, so this is where you have to go."

When I finally realized this, it was a relief. Before I read about this, I assumed Jesus would have had life set up perfectly. That no one in his community would question Him, reject Him, or judge Him. HA! Nothing could be further from the truth. In fact, one of His own disciples (followers) betrayed Him to hand Him over to people who wanted Him dead.

What I learned from this was that if Jesus could be free of letting that rejection poison Him, He could help me figure out how to get free from rejection as well. Even if our families are a certain way, we don't have to be. Even if our friends betray us, we don't have to embrace that betrayal as our identity. Even if no one around us believes in our destiny, even if they talk badly about us, we do not have to nurture and water poisonous areas in our hearts.

What Jesus showed me is that we don't have to be born in a mansion with servants and the best family line, with the most resources, and have everyone love us in order to have a strong and healthy identity. He was able to form His identity apart from others' judgments.

He showed us a new way: that by being connected to the Heavenly Father, you can start to live your best life, destiny, and purpose, in spite of any rejection. There's still opportunity and potential for us if we trust God more than others. The power lies in our hands. It just depends on how willing we are to believe God more than people.

This doesn't mean we won't still need some ideas and skills to help us get from Point A to Point B. There are a few practical ways I believe we can start to heal that sense of rejection so we can start to live a free and empowered life.

Healing Rejection through Community

The first antidote to rejection is community. My sense of being cared for came through community. Community is a healthy group of peers or friends with whom you are safe to be real, open, and yourself—safe to grow. My first real sense of community came from the basketball teams I played on, but yours doesn't have to be sports. Just getting around people who share the same passions and motivations is part of community. You can be in a book club, gardening club, church, anything. Just get with people who care about you, who are willing to walk with you, and want to be with healthy people just as you do. These communities offer you an ecosystem to grow and mature even when you fall flat on your face.

When you are in a healthy community, those friends want to help you dream and express your heart. Community is being around people who won't tear you down (or tear others down in front of you). In community, we inherit principles, establish trust, and plant healthy seeds in the soil of relationships.

Even to Jesus, community is a very big deal. Just look at the twelve disciples He picked. Each one had a different sphere of influence, and different backgrounds. He brought these people together for the greatest journey of their lives. You better believe that, despite bumping heads at times, they were living in community. One of the best ways to counterbalance rejection, especially for a young person, is to discover, connect with, or create a healthy community.

We want to be in community with others we can share our hearts with; people who are going to champion us; people who are not going to mislead us; people who are not going to tear us down; people who will not hold us hostage to what they think we need to do. Lastly and probably most importantly, being in community with others who will be honest with us not for their gain, but for our growth, will help us move past the barriers rejection has created in our lives.

Now, you can also have a community that sets a negative example. If you're running with the wrong crowd, it can set the narrative for your life and the agenda for your calling in a bad way. Those people can cause you to feel even more rejected. If you're surrounding yourself with a positive community, hopefully the people in it are going to steer you in the right direction. They will encourage you to do something positive with your life, something productive and meaningful, while helping you establish a positive identity. In short, they will tell you the actual truth about yourself that is higher than the truth of rejection, and will help you discover the best way to live.

Healing Rejection through Transparency and Values

While I was dating the woman I would later marry, I was living a very promiscuous lifestyle. I was not faithful to her until after we got married. As I stated earlier, a big reason this seed of promiscuity was planted and grew into unfaithfulness was because I was trying to fill the void rejection had created in me with women instead of God's acceptance and love. I didn't even know that was an option.

Once, not long after getting married, God spoke to my heart and said I had to tell my wife about the women I had been with before committing to marriage. That scared me!!! I thought, "Well, I'm about to lose my wife, then! Dang, if I tell her all of this, I will lose her for sure!"

At the time, I was just starting my journey with God. But I felt like He said, "Do you trust Me?" I did, even though I was scared out of my mind. Things were going well in our new marriage; we had peace without arguing. But because I trusted God, I told her.

As you can imagine, things got REALLY rocky, and I was in the doghouse for a VERY long time! It was not easy for my wife to hear that, of course, and not easy for me, either. I had to keep fighting against going back into shame-and-rejection mode about myself. However, telling her brought us closer in the end. Why? Because that area had now been exposed to the light, and there was no more room for shame, fear of rejection, or going back to that behavior to grow in me. I received the greatest freedom in trusting God with the most precious thing to me: my wife and family.

The roots of deception, promiscuity, and secrecy got dug up and thrown out of my life because I did what God asked me to do. I learned that when you bring things to light, you can overcome them. When you are honest, that weakness you struggled with no longer has power to control you or set you up for future torment. Attacks come against you in dark areas because these are where we hide and experience shame. We all fall short, but God does not attack us for it. When we admit our wrongdoings, we get to receive His grace and work toward becoming the new creation He has called us to be. This is what a person of faith would refer to as "repentance."

If we keep things in the dark or hide them, it allows roots of bitterness, fear, and unhealthy identity to manifest and grow even bigger in our lives. Unhealthy and destructive thoughts, patterns, or false beliefs start to develop. They make the void grow bigger, whereas if we bring them into the light and allow the Lord to start to heal us inside, we will start to see a healthy transformation in our lives. Being vulnerable is not easy; however, it's one of the most powerful and liberating things we can do to bring change in our lives.

I believe most people feel more connected with us and trust us more deeply when we are honest about our downfalls than when we are boasting about our triumphs. Seeing your triumph despite your downfalls can give them hope. So when I did that with my wife, I received victory *and* it made it easier to help others later. I could say, "Man, I struggled with that, too! And man, if I got a breakthrough, then I know there's breakthrough for you as well."

To heal rejection, we have to learn how to express our heart and where we're at with our community. For me this was a huge hurdle to get around, as I was always told not to reveal my emotions. But if we are able to let our guard down with the right people, it actually brings out the best in us!

A positive community will hold you accountable and help you become transparent. This is a key to growing as a person: having positive transparent role models who can give you some type of target to aim for in your progression of growth as an individual.

That accountability should be positive, without creating fear or condemnation. It should not cause us to keep things in the dark or be ashamed of our shortcomings. Accountability is exactly that: it's an *account* of your *ability*, for all you can potentially be and do in life.

No one can help if no one knows what you're going through. People want to support you, even if you don't feel supported in your own home. There were a lot of times growing up when I did not feel support from my mom. It's not because she didn't love me or care about me. She was going through a lot herself. She was often in survival mode as she was trying to keep food on the table. I love my mom; she is amazing!

However, she was not able to provide for all the areas of my heart, and I needed a community to hold me up. I think one of the main reasons I didn't become a statistic or fall into crime or other destructive things is that I had a basketball community.

Even if the people in your community do not know God, they may recognize some of His values and characteristics—like doing positive things, uplifting people, or establishing deep trust. A community that's going to allow you to grow is worth investing your time in. Those relationships have the potential to be long-lasting and deep.

In a community, it's not about just you, it's about helping others around you as well. It's about growing your heart and helping others do the same. When we make mistakes, it's about being honest, then lifting each other up, not tearing others down.

If we start becoming cocky and unteachable, these are the people who will be honest with us and hold us accountable for our attitude. We give them permission, as I say, to "keep it 100 with you," as in 100 percent honest.

Why is transparency so important? Because one way we remove

the roots of bitterness and rejection in our lives is by bringing those things to the surface. The Bible says that darkness cannot dwell where light is (John 1:5). If you have roots of bitterness and rejection in your life, and those are in the dark, they are less likely to heal, and more likely to cause much pain in our lives.

Maybe there's something in your past that still has power to cause you to feel rejected and unworthy. You may make a mistake, or many of them, in your community. Bringing that to light is the first step toward your freedom and breakthrough. I know this is sometimes easier said than done. If it was easy, everyone would be living in the fullness of their identity, but they clearly are not.

This always makes me think of King David in the Bible. He endured some very dark hours in his life, and the psalms he wrote are full of his pain and anguish. David murdered, lied, and cheated. He did some really bad things, but he understood the power of repentance and bringing things to the light.

He understood the power of repentance and worship, and God redeemed him in that. The Bible says our worship is a spiritual weapon of warfare. Instead of hiding his sin, David was honest about it. And God walked with him through his wrongs because David owned it, outed himself, and acknowledged what he had done. God forgave him and then said David was a man after His heart. Even if people did not forgive Him, God did!

So God's invitation for us is to constantly pursue that place of peace with Him, where we can be one with Him even when we fall short. That gives me hope, and I pray it does the same for you.

Healing Rejection through Relationship with God

This brings me to the third way to heal rejection. I had to come to know that God was my Father and the truth of what He thinks about me, then to believe that truth. God's Word really helped me learn this. Not religion, but to know God as a father and to know that He wanted to be close to me, even if others didn't.

This wasn't the most natural thing for me. Again, you have to understand I don't know my dad till this day. I have never experienced having the love of a father. It was foreign to me. I felt being abandoned, shamed, forgotten, and hurt. My idea of a father was one of emptiness and pain, not acceptance and love. So it took everything in me to want to walk on the journey of healing and receiving God's love. But it was the best *yes* I ever said in my life.

I discovered He doesn't want a religious experience for us, He wants a relational one—and that's where I was broken, in understanding how to be in healthy relationships. To fully heal rejection, I had to open up to hear God's truth. That's where God came in and plucked some of those thorns of rejection and uprooted the toxic seeds that were in my heart. He plucked them out, and I started getting healed.

The more we get to know God and the closer we get to Him, the easier it is to reject the rejection we might have taken on in the past. To know that we're not designed to be perfect, we're designed to be one with Him. To be intentional in our relationship with God is our highest and most fulfilling calling. We get the privilege of leaning on Him for guidance and to set the true narrative for our lives.

A healthy identity stems from knowing what God says about you. This also helps us be better people in our communities; it also helps others see what transparency is. When we have a healthy identity in God, we can admit that we are wrong. We are able to be open and transparent without feeling condemned, judged, or ridiculed. He is perfect, so we don't have to be. We know God (Jesus) died for our sins and mistakes so that we could be free in Him.

God's original design for us is that we would be one with Him in our identity. We would have no shame in ourselves because we are in Him. I think all the way back to Genesis, when Adam and Eve were walking with God. Their identity was fully in Him and who He made them to be. They were walking around the garden completely naked, and then they ate fruit from the tree God said not to eat from. Only then did they come to realize they were naked, and covered themselves up.

I think at that point they were looking to cover up more than their bodies. They became ashamed of being naked because their union and oneness with God, based on how He saw them, was broken. As soon as sin set in and separated them from God, the identity crisis occurred and shame started.

It all stemmed from the number one sin in the Bible: "Don't eat the fruit of that tree." But they ate it because they were persuaded to question who God was, who He said they were, and what He called them to do. This is when the pain of rejection started. Later, Adam and Eve had a son who killed another because of rejection.

They stepped out of their true identity into rejecting God and His Word. This, in turn, separated them from God, which made them lose access to both Him and their own sense of identity. Once they bought into that lie, they gave away the number one thing their identity was rooted in, which was unity with God.

God's original design for our identity is that we would be one with Him. So when hard times come, that's how you combat them.

Jesus had a strong sense of identity. When He began His ministry, we read that the enemy came to tempt Him, offering Him kingdoms and all kinds of things. But Jesus did something really profound. He said what God said. He spoke out God's own Word against the enemy. That is a blueprint for us to take note of.

That is how we combat the lies of the enemy. The enemy wants to steal our identity and understanding of how God designed us, which is to be one with Him. But by knowing what God says about us, we can overcome. Learning who we are in God will also keep us from accepting the temptation of a lesser-than life.

It is important to realize the enemy tried to attack Jesus's identity with a half-truth. He even used pieces of Scripture taken out of context. He said, "If you bow down and worship me, I'll give you all these things." And he showed him all the kingdoms of this world in an instant.

The enemy tried to get him to exchange a Kingdom with no end, which already belonged to Him, for a kingdom that was temporary. Jesus obviously hit him with a scripture, saying, "It is written..." Jesus had a response based on what He knew from His relationship with the Father.

That's what the world will sometimes offer you—little bits and pieces out of truth for you to buy into. But the fact is, anything that takes you away from God has the potential to hurt you and leave you empty.

Lack of identity is so painful and destructive. Jesus came to make a way to heal that rejection so we can be reconnected to our purpose and identity in life: to be one with God.

I don't want you to think everything will be easy. Things are going to be hard. God's Word actually says that (2 Timothy 3:1). It's a real grind to really be faithful to what God wants to do in your life. There's a lot of temptation out there, just like what Jesus was offered—the world is full of "quick fixes." The price of those quick fixes is that you lose your purpose and identity, and you get separated from the One who really has a greater destiny in mind for you.

As you become one with God and serve people, you see the goodness of God over your life, over your purpose, and how much you can impact others. If you're focused on His agenda first, you live from peace and purpose.

Matthew 6:33 says if you seek the kingdom first and all His righteousness, everything else will be added unto you—your peace, your purpose, your journey. Even if you're having a nervous breakdown, if you know where to get your strength from, you know

He will bring you out of it.

Once we have a real revelation and understanding of who God says we are, gone are the days where we have to feel rejected or inferior. We get to hear a new narrative of acceptance in our heart, and that empowers us to live a higher and more fulfilling life than anything else

CHAPTER
five

{ A Grounded
Identity }

S o, how can we start to recognize when we and others have overcome rejection in our identities?

Some indicators are that we can now resist the temptation to let others script our narratives. We can also resist the temptation to define ourselves by our mistakes. When we are healthy, we can have hope even when we make mistakes because we know they don't define us. We still have peace. We still have purpose in God. Our narrative is not determined by anything or anyone but Him.

Having a healthy identity means we are able to admit when we're were wrong and apologize to others. In that way, we are able to maintain relationships and be healthy people others can relate to. We are able to listen even when we disagree, and to disagree in a healthy and respectful way. We don't have to lash out or shrink back, but we can articulate what's in our hearts and share our views and feelings. This happens when we really start not only to gain wisdom, but more importantly, to move in that wisdom to bring peace in sensitive situations. If someone doesn't receive or accept that peace, we can remain unperturbed in our hearts because we know who God is and who we are. This allows us to bless and love people even when we don't agree with them.

I think the number one indicator of a healthy identity is knowing and being content with what God says about you, and continually agreeing with it—especially when it is hard and "the rubber meets the road" for you, like it did for Jesus in the Garden of Gethsemane. This allows us to stay grounded in our hearts, dreams, emotions, thoughts, and actions.

Grounded in Our Hearts
The first step to being grounded in our hearts is to start a dialogue with God by speaking to Him. What??!! Yep, that's right—spend time opening up your heart to Him and sharing what's on your mind. The religious word for that process is "prayer." But what if you're not

religious? What if you don't understand religion? What if your idea of faith is wrapped up in religious rules?

Well, I have news for you: Jesus wasn't religious, either. As a matter of fact, some of the people Jesus had problems with were the religious leaders. He was trying to rewire their hearts because they saw God as an oppressive lawmaker and portrayed Him that way to the people. But Jesus came to be a servant and to show what unconditional love looks like. In Matthew 20:28, He said that "the Son of Man did not come to be served, but to serve, and to give His life as a ransom for many." He came as God in the flesh, and the religious people totally missed Him. They totally missed the Kingdom of God.

Asking God into your heart establishes the foundation for your greatest core values—values on which entire generations of your family can build. God is eternal; He has plans for eternity. The beauty of those plans is that He wants us to actively participate with them! If our treasure is in temporary things, our hearts will be fickle. But when we understand that our treasure lies in discovering all He has for our lives, we find out that the plans for our lives are great and mighty.

The next step is to ask God to show you parts of your heart that may have been hurt, betrayed, misled, or even damaged—the parts that need repair, care, restoration, or replenishment. Ask Him to show you parts of your heart that are healthy as well, and what would make them even healthier. I encourage you to take heed of what He shows you—and then act on those things! Although it will be challenging, it will be the most liberating thing you ever do.

The damaged parts of our hearts can be fully restored. Any part that is bitter or dead, God can bring back to abundant life. This was HUGE for me. There were times when I was angry, and I didn't even know why. I would lash out at people I loved. I was confused about why I would react in such a way. I was even more confused about why I was so cynical.

The narrative of the world was taking a toll on me, and I wasn't even aware of it. However, when I discovered God, He helped me see how those things were taking root in my heart. He helped me to see that there was hope daily to see the change in my life that I desired. He has that same hope for you if you desire to it for yourself

Before I really, fully let God into my heart, I thought I was doing fine, and that if I was a good person, that alone would qualify me. When a real test came, that did not work. Knowing our Father is a heart process, not a head process. Religion is a head process. I had a heart that was not pure or steadfast. And I failed—big time. My heart was not secure or grounded; it was still full of bitterness, fear, and loss, and it was leading me in a deceptive way. At times, even now, those things try to stir back up—so I constantly remind myself of the new life I have inherited.

I'm constantly finding things about myself and about my heart that God is repairing in His grace. He's always digging around in my roots and grounding me more deeply in who I'm called to be, what I'm called to do, and how I'm supposed to impact and influence the world. He wants to do the same things for you. My desire is that as you continue to read, that hope will give you strength as well.

If our hearts are rooted in Him, we will start to see that He loves us. His love will fill up the voids, answer the questions, and calm our fears. We will start to understand that we are called by Him. He designed us. We will realize that there is great and tremendous potential, not only for us, but for the rest of the world around us. He gives us eternal hope.

When our hearts are grounded in God, we start to see ourselves as He sees Himself in us. He sees there is no ceiling for us—only the one we put on ourselves. Proverbs 4:23 says, "Above all else, guard your heart for everything you do, everything you do flows from it." If you are doing negative things, it likely means a piece (or the majority) of your heart is hurt. The good news is that God has a major purpose and plan for your heart and for your life. He can do emotional heart surgery if we allow Him access to our deepest hurt and pain.

We also can ask God to bring healing by simply renewing our hearts! There's nothing that can push or shake us out of what God has called us to do. Jeremiah 33:3 says, "Call to Me, and I will answer you, and show you great and mighty things, which you do not know." When you feel like you do not know what to do, you can ask God. He will always be there to remind you and tell you great things. He's constantly trying to have a relationship with us, and He loves to remind us of that!

Grounded in Our Dreams

There are two kinds of dreams we have: the ones when we are awake and hoping for something, and the ones we have when we are asleep. In this book, I am focusing on dreams we have when we are awake. These could also be described as hopes or goals.

Before I knew God, my dreams were full of despair and lack. Sometimes, I felt more defeated than encouraged when I set goals. I felt empty and misguided. I didn't think there would ever going to be a time when I would be happy because of the void in my heart.

Initially, my dream was to go to college, get a degree, and then play professional sports. I achieved those dreams. Part of me wanted to do it to get back at people (even some of my family) for saying that I couldn't. I wanted to prove them wrong. That was the wrong motive, and even though I achieved my goal, it hindered my growth as a person. I did it all with this huge chip of resentment on my shoulder instead of pursuing my goals with joy and passion.

Because of that, when things got really rough, I didn't have confidence that anyone else could help me even when they believed in me and my dream. So I felt very isolated and very alone. It was a "me against the world" mentality, which at times worked, but never led to happiness. It caused my heart to harden and stunted my relationship skills. It also prevented me from understanding how to accept healthy advice from others without labeling them as haters or people who didn't want me to succeed.

When I found God and I submitted my dreams, ambitions, and thought life to Him, He started to change the foundation I operated from in life. When I say I "submitted" them, let me clarify: Some people do not like the word "submit"; they see it as weakness. Actually, to submit is a good thing when the person you are submitting to has your best interest in mind. In sports, I was used to this. I submitted to my coaches and to my team. I didn't make my own plans and just go for it. The times I did do that, I failed really badly! If I thought there was a good play we could develop in practice, I might submit that idea to the team. If I was double-teamed and my teammate was wide open by the hoop, I wouldn't try to take a shot myself. I would submit to what was best for the team and pass the ball to my teammate. But ultimately, it was the coach or the team that decided. They had the experience to know more than I knew.

God is the most perfect Coach that has ever existed! He doesn't just know *some* plays, He knows them all. He knows how to get us out of situations we wouldn't have a clue about. He knows how to get us into a life we could never dream of! So as I submitted to His game plan for life, He started to reveal some areas of my heart that I thought were helping me, but in actuality they were hurting me. He started to show me that real growth and happiness started by being in a relationship with Him, and learning from that how to be in relationship with others.

This impacted my heart so much that I started coaching at a local high school in a very, very small town in Washington state. I started serving the kids in that community, which in turn gave me access to the families in that community, which allowed me access to their hearts. That transformed my life and brought in authentic peace, purpose, and happiness. More importantly, I discovered something really beneficial for daily living: serving others.

That time of coaching primed me to be a pastor, and pastoring is preparing me for something even greater in God! I have yet to discover what that is; however, I have been enjoying the journey and have so much peace in it. I have a sense that nothing in my past was wasted, and God is working all things for good as I pursue the dreams He has for me.

When you are grounded in your dreams, it means you know they have eternal impact, and are not just for you. A dream that is grounded and stable is a dream that is meant to impact the people and world around you. It will impact and change culture and society. It will also bring insight to others who are searching for the goals and calling for their lives.

One of my first dreams was to be a great dad. I believe God put that dream in my heart when I was a child, and it has stuck with me. God actually blessed me with that. I am still a work in progress, as we all are; however, progress is proceeding in the right direction.

A few years ago, I wanted to do and be more for my family. I dreamed of finding an environment that would help me become a better husband to my wife, a better dad to my kids, and better person and leader in my community. That dream came from the heart of God. It was grounded in His eternal heart for my life.

About four years later, I got an opportunity to work at a church in San Diego, California, and that has given me phenomenal opportunities to learn and to grow. I grew closer to God, learned more about myself, and learned more of what it means to really love others, with no agenda other than reflecting God to them through my life.

One of my dreams now is to travel around the world to counsel influencers and leaders in different nations, inspiring them to use it to impact the world for the glory of God. I want to help these leaders and nations adopt Kingdom values and principles that they can implement to see healthy change in their economies, citizens, families, and children. Most would say this is a very audacious dream, but I know that if it comes from the heart of God and is meant to serve others, He will make a way for it to come to pass.

I believe you have big dreams that God wants to partner with as well. How much does it glorify God, help others, and set up generational opportunity? If you start there, you are well on your way to seeing it fulfilled. You will be grounded along the way and fulfilled with authentic purpose.

That is not to say that challenges, temptations, and distractions won't come. They sometimes even come disguised as opportunities!! However, as you dig deeply into who God says you are, you gain more clarity along the way.

I think about Joseph in the Bible when I think of dreams. He had a dream about how much he was going to influence his family and nation. His dream came true, but at first there was a lot of arrogance behind it, and as a result, he took the long road into the fullness of his dream. But when he started to use his dream-interpretation skills to serve people, his own dream came true.

Being grounded in your dream is agreeing with God about it and knowing how it will benefit your community, your friends, and your family. Those dreams are blessings for other people as well—the kind that will bring you life and fulfillment. These are the kinds of dreams that can ground you and keep your focus strong enough to overcome challenges as you work to see your dream come to pass.

Grounded in Our Emotions

There are emotional parameters we need that allow us to continually grow on our journey without getting distracted. Establishing parameters around our emotions and the people who impact us helps us to step into a greater version of ourselves. We start to have confidence in God's Word, and it brings a peace that passes all our understanding. It brings emotional security and strength. More importantly it can do so even in the darkest moments in our lives.

Being grounded may require us to establish emotional parameters that allow for healthy growth, such as taking time to play or rest. You need to know how you take care of yourself and be aware of your physical, emotional, and mental intake and output (i.e., "garbage in, garbage out"). When you refuse to put yourself in environments that cause your emotions to spin out of control, you will go places, do things, and converse in ways that demonstrate grounded emotions. Those emotional parameters are very important because they allow the roots of your spirit to grow even deeper into the calling God has for your life.

What you don't want is become arrogant. No one wants to be around people like that! Their parameters are selfish and do not glorify God or offer hope to others. Being grounded in healthy environments establishes our emotions, which should naturally benefit people around us. Others may not necessarily see that right away, but that gives us an opportunity to help them understand the importance of what we're doing. Our journey of personal growth offers an invitation for them to have the same thing in their lives.

The beauty of having a relationship with the Lord is that you can ask the Holy Spirit to help keep your emotions grounded; the Bible says He is our Counselor. He tells us what we are doing well, and He tells us things that we lack. That's good news for all of us if we desire healthy growth.

Growing up in a fatherless home meant I was exposed to some things about sex that I deemed to be love—but it was only lust. So my emotions, ideas, thoughts, and values about women and sex were ungrounded and unhealthy. God helped me discover this and that I had no resistance or sense of accountability in those areas. I realized everything I thought was romantic love was just lust wrapped up in very self-centered thoughts and ideals.

God had to show that to me—but then He started to counsel me. He helped me create healthy boundaries around my heart and helped me discover what love looks like from His perspective. He redeemed and healed me of those things so I could be a better person to the people I cared for. No longer would those emotions mislead me or hurt others.

Grounded in Our Thoughts

In order to be grounded in our thoughts, we have to know and be grounded in God's thoughts. How do we do that? Through His Word! We need to find out who He says we are and agree with that in our own minds. The greatest way to see if we are grounded in our thoughts is to see if they are bringing us, or people around us, harm or stagnation, or whether they are causing us to have more abundant life and inspiring others along the way.

Second Timothy 1:7 says God didn't give us a spirit of fear, but of power, love, and a sound mind. Some other translations say "self-discipline." Our thoughts should be grounded in the truth of what God thinks about us, what He says about us, and what He wants for us. Only then will our minds be sound, despite all the noise and opinions around us.

Just like any other discipline, we have to practice! If you want to be in shape, you're going to eat right, exercise, and be disciplined in that area of your life. If you want to be a professional athlete, you're going to do the training, run the drills and practice a lot, even when you feel like sleeping or taking a day off. All that training eventually becomes a lifestyle.

If we want to be grounded in our thoughts, we have to start thinking and saying great things as well as God's truth over our lives, day in and day out. And we have to say those things to our household and over our circumstances, even when that seems dumb or impossible. When we push through with the established disciplines we've learned to practice, they help us live from victory rather than victimhood.

Doing that means we are declaring our lives and our circumstances are under God's control, that God is faithful, and that God is working on our hearts and protecting them. When we learn how to place everything in God's hands, we start to see His hand in everything! When we are grounded in the knowledge that we have a Heavenly Father who's listening to us, who wants to walk alongside us, who wants to help us and protect us, it gives us hope. Even when things feel hopeless, we are able to carry peace and hope when others cannot.

My mother loved me and my family, and I always felt like there was promise and potential for me. I grounded my heart and my thoughts to press forward, to pursue things even when I didn't know what it was going to look like. At that time I didn't even have a relationship with God, and really didn't believe in Him much. However, I did believe in hope. Honestly, that is all I had.

I got a college scholarship, went to school, and had my education paid for through my talent. This helped me stay focused and disciplined in those areas of my life. But as I mentioned, there will always be moments of limitation and failure in our minds when they are not rooted in God. They have the ability to distract us and derail our passions and dreams. When things got hard, I crumbled. Have you ever felt that way?

When I found Christ, I found that if I rooted my thoughts in Him and what He said about me, even when things got really, really difficult I still had peace. I had focus. As a result, it impacted the people around me for good, even when they were telling me I was going the wrong way or wasn't seeing things right. I stayed true to what I discovered in giving my life to God.

I love what Philippians 4:8 says: "Finally, brethren, whatever things are true, whatever things *are* noble, whatever things *are* just, whatever things *are* pure, whatever things *are* lovely, whatever things *are* of good report, if *there is* any virtue and if *there is* anything praiseworthy—meditate on these things." Basically, think about things that bring peace and purpose to your life.

Colossians 3:1 says, "If then you were raised with Christ, seek those things which are above, where Christ is, sitting at the right hand of God." Why? Because the world and earthly things will let you down. The world will reject you and say you are less than, even cancel you. Yet, if you stand up for truth, that helps people to grow and offer hope to others around them. This is the start of true identity in God. One way we do this is knowing what He is already speaking about us through His Word.

If we allow the world to dictate our mindset, we can open our hearts up to the hurt that inhabits the world, not the blessing and freedom that God has for our lives. But when we are grounded, even in the midst of uncertainty we can be certain in God and ask Him to help us, rather than being bullied by the thought of "being canceled."

Grounded in Agreement and Action
Ultimately, if we are going to live a victorious life, we need to know what God says about us. (We will discuss this in more detail in the next chapter.) We also need to be willing to agree with God instead of resisting Him.

In the Bible, there is a story about a man named Naaman. He contracted leprosy, which, if you have never heard of this disease, is absolutely brutal. It eats the flesh, and in Jesus's day, the people who had it were social outcasts who had to stay a certain distance away from everyone around them. They were socially distant before "social distancing" was ever created! The people who had it were forced to live in colonies outside of town.

One of Naaman's servants was an Israelite girl who was captured in battle. He suggested that Naaman visit a prophet of God (a person who could hear God's voice) to receive healing. Naaman listened to her and took her advice.

But he got frustrated as it all rolled out. Naaman got upset because the prophet told him to go into the dirty, filthy water of the Jordan River and wash. Naaman thought his healing would come from a prayer or blessing, not a bath in filthy water! He had to learn that his blessing was wrapped in his agreement—and when he was willing to accept and agree with God's word, he was healed.

Getting that healing took following the advice of someone the world deemed "less than" and doing what God told him to do even though it was uncomfortable. But when he did, he was healed and blessed—and that young servant's life probably changed from that point forward as well.

Our greatest blessing is wrapped in our agreement with and obedience to God. Just look at what happened with me and my wife! That blessing of our relationship came out of being willing to listen, agree, and act. That was SOOO hard at the time! But that story now provides great breakthrough for many others who struggled as I did.

God may tell you to do certain things. And sometimes it won't make sense, like it didn't make sense to Naaman or to me when God told me to tell my wife about the other women I had been with before we were married. In both examples, obedience partnered with faith released blessing, maturity, and destiny—which paved the way for truth and life to develop in me.

Ultimately, God knows what we need more than we do, and when we agree, we are healed. When we find and invest in a community, when we are transparent and willing to get feedback, and when we obey God—even when it doesn't make sense—we are well on our way to leaving rejection in the dust and operating from a sense of identity, peace, and power in life!

CHAPTER
six

A New
Narrative

O n my journey, I quickly learned that I had to trade the old narrative I had about myself for the narrative that comes from God. As I did this, I discovered the truth about my identity. So what is this narrative that comes from God?

I know you know what the world says about you! It usually sucks! It usually tells you that you are not good enough, that you are inferior, and that you have to earn love, acceptance, and appreciation— mainly by changing yourself to be someone others like. Sometimes that narrative will try to "cancel" you within our culture.

The narrative that comes from God is the opposite. It says you are loved and worthy of love. When someone feels loved, despite their faults and failures, it actually brings out the best in them! God's narrative tells you that even though you are not enough, Jesus died to give you access to everything in life as if you were enough. You have access to opportunity, resources, and people as if you were enough.

I have seen people accept the narrative from God to varying degrees. Some people stay at a certain level of experiencing God's love, and that is not bad. That is a great first step. As I mentioned in the last chapter, this is not based on what God gives, but on how much we accept and how much we are willing to sacrifice our old thinking.

The difference between these two things is profound. Anyone can have an experience with God, but those experiences don't always progress into having an encounter with God. But when we encounter God, we actually dive into understanding what it is to be a loved son or daughter on a daily basis.

An experience is memorable. For example, when I coached with the Seattle SuperSonics, that was an experience. I was a part of the team, and that was incredible! But did it change me on a deep level and start uprooting my old narratives about myself? Not so much. Similarly, you may have eaten a great meal or visited a theme park.

It was great—but when it was over, it was over. It didn't change you, even though you remember it fondly. Many people who attend church may be at this level of experiencing God.

An encounter is different. An encounter transforms you. You start to evolve and transform over time. An encounter changes how you see yourself, how you see others, how you see your future, how you see the world, etc.

An experience is watching a great football game. An encounter is being drafted onto a football team. Encounters give you fresh vision and hope. The great thing about God is that encounters with Him are not like getting drafted because you don't have to earn anything. It is a gift; we just have to accept it.

The encounter I had with God when I was at work that day became a foundation for my life going forward. It changed everything about my life. And I have encouraging news: An encounter with God can do the same for you as well!!

These kinds of transformational encounters have been happening for centuries. A guy named Saul had an encounter with Jesus thousands of years ago. Mind you, it wasn't necessarily the most pleasant encounter; it temporarily blinded him. (SHEESH!) But it put him on a trajectory to step into what he was called to do, which was to impact the masses.

Just think about this: Saul was a Jew and an expert on Judaism. He went around killing and tormenting Christians (followers of Christ) until he had this encounter. You would think that once he gave his life to Christ, he would speak to all the Jewish people about Jesus. But God essentially told him, "I'm going to use you in the opposite way people think I would."

And then, Saul's name was changed to Paul and he became an apostle (leader) to anyone who was not Jewish (the Gentiles). At first, the Christians of the time were still scared of him and wanted nothing to do with him. But after that encounter, Paul's identity was so firmly rooted in Christ that nothing anyone did could stop him. His expertise in Judaism was used to serve a group that didn't want anything to do with Judaism! That is just crazy and demonstrates the depths of his inward encounter. Man would not take that route— but God did. More significantly, it shows that God's grace can reach the "un-reachable"—even murderers and those who seek to harm others to the greatest possible degree.

God makes it clear in His Word that He can use anybody, even if we have a background that makes us think we are the opposite of what is needed, wanted, or desirable for a task. We can't put God in a box, because when He encounters us, it is outside of the box. He can call you into anything and empower you to get there. The most amazing thought is the one God has already had about you, even if you feel like you don't qualify in His eyes!!

The Bible says, "For I know the thoughts that I think toward you, says the LORD, thoughts of peace and not of evil, to give you a future and a hope" (Jeremiah 29:11). It's so encouraging that we have a future and hope even if we have failed in certain areas of our lives! Our grasp of that future and hope may not look the way we initially envisioned it, but that doesn't mean it isn't a blessing for our lives.

When we have an encounter, we don't have to accept the synthetic love the world offers us; we can have eternal love. We don't have to accept what others may see as our future—like "you can't go to college," "you can't make something yourself," "you can't have a family," "you can't love your wife," "you can't make love to your wife," etc. We don't have to accept these things just because we were not guided correctly in these areas or given the opportunity to grow in them when we were young.

Think about Saul again for a moment. What have you done that you feel might disqualify you from getting a new narrative from God?

Saul murdered Christians. Talk about being on the wrong path in life! Talk about something Christians would have said meant he would amount to nothing good. But then, the very group that he was murdering accepted him as one of its leaders!

Think about that! If, for example, a Taliban leader who was actively hunting down the members of the group you were connected with later declared he wanted to join your group, would you want him as your leader? Would you have the courage to trust that person? The only way you would be able to do that would be if you truly saw that person's life had been genuinely changed. That's the difference between experience and encounter. Experience is memorable, but encounter is transformative!

God can change hearts—and when God has a plan, no man, woman, or circumstance can stop it. People might say that murdering God's people disqualified Saul from writing a big part of the Bible and taking the Lord's message to many parts of the world. But God did not say that; it was actually the opposite. So, no matter what your background is or what people might think of you, there is redemption, freedom, and a greater truth possible for you through an encounter with God!

Traveling Light
It seems to me that the deeper you go with God, the less you can take along on your journey, and the better the journey gets. It requires less of your own thinking, less of your own understanding, less of what you believe based on your limited experience of life and the world. It's almost as if He requires you to abandon all those things in order to travel light with Him.

Anytime you take a trip somewhere, it's always easier to travel with less baggage or things. It's the same with our faith: the more comfortable we get with abandoning all our old thinking, speech, and way of life, the more God can fill us up with the things we actually need while we are on our journey with Him.

Now, we may feel we deserve the right to carry the baggage of what others have done to us or how they have treated us. But that's like saying, "I deserve the right to carry around the trash of the world with me everywhere I go." Really? I mean, we can choose to do that, but how is that helping us? It is not! It is only weighs us down—and worse, it guarantees that everywhere we go, stuff stinks!

It's like insisting on wearing old, used, dirty rags instead of receiving the privilege of wearing a new set of clothes. More than that, it's like hoping people will value, pursue, and appreciate you wearing the rags. I spent years trying to get some kind of validation and appreciation for the rags I was wearing, when I didn't realize it was actually getting me the opposite!

It is incredibly liberating to let go of our baggage. The more we give to Him, the easier it is for us to find His truth for ourselves. What does He want to give us instead? He wants to give us a life where we feel joy, peace, goodness, and self-control instead of being controlled by others. Freedom comes from getting closer to Him, and as we do, He gives us strength to not allow pain, fear, or rejection to have power over us. Freedom also affords us the ability to have hope in low seasons of our lives.

This is what it means to encounter true love. The encounter changes us in all these ways and empowers us with upgrades, gives us the chances we never had, and second chances on the ones we misused. It infuses us with hope when the world says we should not have any based on our situations. God comes in, fills the gaps with truth, and takes you down paths you may not be qualified for. Just going to church doesn't transform your life, but surrendering to Jesus does. And so when you surrender to Jesus, you surrender to love, and that love establishes a fresh starting point for a new destiny for our lives.

Love Tells You the Way and the Truth

Jesus embodied the truth. We know a lot of people claim to know the truth, but He actually personified it. He holds the truth about us, about the world, and about people and situations in our lives! His truth is greater than ours. His truth is greater than that of our friends and family and community. His truth is greater than the truth of our past.

Since I accepted Him, my life has been so different, NO DOUBT! My family is different, my goals are different. My principles are different. My core values are different. I have started to live by different truths that empower me. These things are available to you as well.

Discovering Jesus was the truth and the way wiped away a lot of pain for me. I no longer had to do a lot of things in order to feel accepted and loved. John 16:13 says, "However, when He, the Spirit of truth, has come, He will guide you into all truth; for He will not speak on His own *authority*, but whatever He hears He will speak; and He will tell you things to come."

That's the encounter I had when the Spirit of God showed up while at my work the night I gave my life to Him. He guided me to the starting point of truth, and I embarked upon this journey to fill the void in my heart that I hadn't even known existed.

Before then, I had no idea what real love looked like. No idea what being affirmed felt like. And I thought I had to clamor for attention and acceptance. In receiving Christ, the Spirit of Truth came in and guided me into all truth. His truth was that I no longer needed to be ashamed of anything, and I am so grateful for this breakthrough. This is available to you as well.

In the past, I didn't just want to do my best. It was like I had to *be* the best. My truth used to be that when I fell short, it meant I wasn't good enough, that no one would want me, that no one would help me. But God's truth is different. It is good to do your best and be excellent, but now there's no need for me to be ashamed of myself when I fall short. That's a very liberating truth to receive!

Second Timothy 2:15 says that we can rightly handle the word of truth. The word of truth is not just the physical Bible; it is our lives and the truth of who God made us to be. That means we can rightly handle our identity and life, and be okay with the fact that we will not make the right decisions all the time. There will be days when we make mistakes, but we can still present ourselves to God as one approved. We're approved by God, and that's sufficient.

This doesn't give us the freedom to embrace bad behavior or indulge in things that don't bring life, but it does give us the opportunity to not focus on our mistakes.

The Truth About Yourself

Truth is part of love. And when we encounter God, we encounter a bigger truth of who we are, how He made us, and who our family is. John 8:32 says, "You shall know the truth, and the truth shall make you free." So, as we get to know who God says we are, we will automatically start to move into freedom.

The Bible also says that He chose us before the foundation of the world. We were not an accident to Him. He chose all of us. This really gives me a lot of hope, and hopefully does the same for you as you read this. I am not an accident that He didn't know what to do with; I didn't take Him by surprise. He prepared things for me before He even started to create the earth! We each have to go on a journey to discover our purpose and mine it out for ourselves. We have to choose to say yes to the journey in order to receive the promises.

When I had my first encounter with God, I knew I wasn't doing well on my own, living by my own truth or the truth of the world. I was on the brink of probably losing my family at least, and maybe even getting into some serious legal trouble.

That encounter really changed my life. It gave me the opportunity to marry my wife, expand my family, and embrace perspective, peace, and purpose. That is not something I could do on my own. I had limited perspective about relationships; my examples weren't the healthiest, and my upbringing wasn't conducive to success. However, a relationship with God gave me hope and an opportunity to improve all those areas.

Learning His truth about me broadened my perspective of what real peace looked like, what real love looked like, what real repair looked like. I learned we can play a part in redeeming things that go wrong in the world by coming into a relationship with Him. It showed me what redemptive power looks like, and that it is tangible. It was an encounter. It wasn't just something I read or heard about and tried to apply. The timing of this encounter basically changed the trajectory of not only my life, but my family's.

Once I stepped into that new truth, I started to step into what I was called to do. It wasn't that I got a position or a title that defined me. In fact, I realized what defined me was simply agreeing with the truth God said about me—giving up my truth of lack for His truth of abundance and love. Once I knew God, I could freely abandon the destructive thoughts and beliefs I had once held.

God says that our identity is in Him, and it is safe there! He also tells us that our old ways can be left behind to make room for new life. "Therefore, if anyone is in Christ, he is a new creation; old things have passed away; behold, all things have become new." (2 Corinthians 5:17)

His truth about our identity is everlasting. It doesn't go away. We can be redeemed and completed in a short amount of time; what would take many years of redemption in our own strength, God can do in a brief amount of time based on our willingness to agree and partner with what He envisions for our lives. I heard another leader say it this way: "We are currently growing at the speed of our own obedience." That brought me a lot of peace. It can do the same for you.

When we operate in our own truth, we find it is only as strong as we are. But God is strong according to what His Word says. He becomes our rock and the anchor that grounds us. We're going to fall, but He won't leave us on the ground.

Now, our identity in Christ is not an open door to an easy life. The difference is, He adds strength to us in difficult times. His Word says, "These things I have spoken to you, that in Me you may have peace. In the world you will have tribulation; but be of good cheer, I have overcome the world" (John 16:33).

If I didn't have God's truth about His plan for me, I probably would have left my family and tried to search for a quick fix when I faced challenges. I would have tried to search for my own answers and tried to make stuff happen according to my own truth—and that probably wouldn't have turned out in my favor! But God's truth pursues us and never becomes void.

The Truth About God

Before my encounter, I knew God as a religious deity, not a fatherly God. I didn't know He was a God who wanted to redeem and heal or a God who is close to me.

Before we encounter God, we often base our idea of Him on who people are or what they say. The staggering truth is that, according to a study released in 2019, 64 percent of African American kids grow up in single-parent homes—and 52 percent of those children are growing up without fathers. The fact that the rest have a dad in their life doesn't mean those are totally healthy situations. How do we expect a young kid to have love for God the Father if their earthly father abandoned or abused them? They'll think their Heavenly Father feels the same way. My encounter with God let me know that I'm not abandoned and that I don't have to be left behind.

Fathers have the privilege of teaching young boys to become men and imparting to them masculinity, strength, confidence, and healthy identity. When a boy has access to this leadership, he is more likely to become productive, positive, and have good core values. It's a father's honor to bring healthy correction, guidance, instruction, and leadership in the home. I am so thankful for single mothers, and what they do to love and raise their children. I am not saying their efforts are inferior to the fathers'. Yet there are certain things that fathers can impart to their children that mothers can't, and vice versa. Having a healthy relationship with a father truly is a treasure.

I didn't have that, so society said there was no hope for me. Believing "I did not get what I needed to be productive and create a positive impact" can push someone onto a trajectory that wasn't meant for their life.

However, the encounter I had with God really brought me into a new space of clarity, purpose, and peace to see that my life was going to make a difference even if the odds were stacked against me. And as I continually aligned myself with His truth, He showed me great leadership principles and core values that would help me. I started to feel hope that I could handle money well, handle success, handle failure, and help others do the same. God came in and filled in the gaps.

So what does this mean for you? Maybe you didn't miss out on having your dad in your life; maybe you didn't have a mother, or you had a bad one. God can also offer the kindness, nurturing, healing, and comfort that is oftentimes exemplified by the loving women in our life. Whatever you missed out on, the truth is that God's love can fill the gaps.

Was it hard for me to trust after feeling hurt and abandoned as a young kid? Of course! Most people think money is the way out, that fame or something else is a way out of their situation. And though those things can contribute to getting out, many people can have fame or money for a time and not know how to sustain it. Their identity does not develop with it; they still do not feel grounded. Ultimately, those things are what I believe people are seeking when they find money and fame. And wow, is it a disappointment when they get to the top of the ladder of success and find those things are still missing!

After I encountered God, I started making decisions from a space of freedom and peace, not fear. I knew I could be strengthened in my life even if things didn't go well, and that changed my perspective. Even when I started to get depressed or sad, I knew God was for me no matter what, and that it was time for me to align my rhythm with His vision for my life.

The Bible says God is love. When I started to build my identity around this, I started to become more unshakable. In 1 Corinthians 13 we read, " Love suffers long *and* is kind ... bears all things, believes all things, hopes all things, endures all things" (verse 4, 7). God could bear with me, no matter what I did? He would suffer or put up with me even when I was being ridiculous and still have hope for my life? Wow! I finally had a truth bigger than my own, saying my life would mean something. That motivated me to better myself and my situation. I was finally able to know the truth about myself, which was greater than any other truth, and it gave me so much freedom, peace, and hope

The Truth About Others

The shift in my mindset came not just from learning the truth about myself, but the truth about others. When something happens in life that is really hard, we who suffer from rejection can tend to blame or resent others. That is natural. When we encounter God, we gain more freedom because we don't have to operate from what others did or did not do. For example, in the past, people's actions made me feel like I was a slave to anger—but now I have the freedom to choose what my response will be. In God's truth, you can always have access to healing, peace, and forgiveness.

No matter what we go through in life or how others treat us, we can know and respond with the highest level of truth. If all we know is abandonment and rejection, we will probably make things worse for ourselves by reacting in anger and pain. It is not wrong to have anger or pain, but when we lash out, it doesn't bring healthy sustainable solutions or change, and it can make things worse. That is a heavy burden. God gives us the option to bring strength into our lives and to others around us.

So now, when I walk in a room, even my enemies have no choice but to see a picture of God through me. They have an opportunity to encounter Christ. Before Christ, my behavior was more hurtful to myself and others; I didn't have control of myself. So how could I expect them to treat me better than I was treating them? That's hypocritical.

Before I met God, when I saw my enemies I would react in rage. How many of them changed their behavior or words because of my reactions? None. HAHA. Not one. I felt like I was doing something powerful in the moment, but at the end of the day, I was just teaching them to avoid me, judge me, ostracize me, or cancel me even more.

But with God, I was able to rise above that perspective of my hurt, to a higher truth—one that actually had power to change people. I started to see that God can use me to help my enemies change—especially if they do not deserve my kindness! He can fight for me, He can defend me, He can protect my heart from hurt, and He can change them, too. I no longer had to live as a victim of hurt, anger, and self-pity.

I didn't realize how these three things were such heavy burdens to me until I started to let them go. I mean, I have not met anyone whose identity is built on hurt and self-pity who is happy, thriving, respected, and doing greater things. Now, I'm not saying it's not a natural response to feel bad for yourself when bad things happen, but God gives us an option that brings life through His greater truth.

The Truth About Your Future

Before my encounter with God, if you had told me that my life was going to work out for the good, I probably would have laughed right in your face. I was a hot mess express rolling down the tracks! But God said, "Nope, all those things I am going to work together for good." And He is saying the same thing about your life, even If you can't see it right now.

Roman 8:28 says all things work together for good for those who are called according to His purpose. And all of us are called! It's just that not all of us respond and start to walk in that calling. But when you have God at the center of your life, His truths start to guide you in the direction you need to go. We come into a place of destiny when we submit our journey to His leading.

This means that no matter what may have happened to us, God has the ability to force some good to come out of it, even if we feel it is impossible. He is the Master Author, and just like superheroes who are shaped by negative events, ours can cause us to overcome and help others live in greater freedom, as we do.

According to Jeremiah 29:11, the Lord has plans to give you a future. And a hope. He knows the plans He has for you. They are always for good. God made you wonderful because He loves you and wants you to have a good future.

Who in the world has promised you a good life and is powerful enough to make it happen? Let's be honest, we all want that—but who actually has that kind of power? We can't be transformed by this world. The world doesn't promise us a good future or hope.

Not at all.

But God says that in Him, we are a new creation! Even when we have done bad things in the past, the Bible says the old things have passed and behold, the new has come. As we follow God, we start to transform into a new version of ourselves that was never possible before! And we see our future more clearly.

How does God change our future to one of hope? Through our agreement. He already has His good future and plans for our lives, but we have to accept it. He is not a bully or an oppressor who forces us to choose Him. He wants us to be empowered to make our own choice. We can choose to love Him, to have abundant life ... or not. It is up to us. God always wants to encounter us, but we have to take a step toward that encounter. When we take one step toward Him, He takes greater ones toward us.

Rebuilding Firm Foundations

God invited me to build a new foundation through a narrative that brought me life and peace. You also can build a foundation on God. When you do, it will not crumble even when you feel you are weak. It will ground you; it will hold you steady on a good course. But, in order for your foundation to be strengthened, you have to put in some work. If you accept Jesus, He will lay a new foundation for you.

The problem is: the cement of our foundation may still be wet, and we may be stepping in it, sinking into it, wanting to still bring our own ideas about our past and our old identity into it. That is normal and there is no shame in it, but the more we are willing to let go of, the more we can actually transform and see that our foundation is sure. It's not that God is calling us out. He's actually calling us up into our greatness in Him. He is helping us see how we need to take out the garbage so we don't stink! The main thing needed for that cement to dry and strengthen and keep you grounded is to depart from the old things that were keeping you unstable.

An opportunity for long-term success, can be built if we embrace establishing our life on the words God says in the Bible and link them directly to our hearts. Luke 6 discusses the several ways to build a house. One man dug deep and laid his foundation on the rock. When a storm and waves came against the house it did not shake because it was well-built deep down into the rock. That house is a picture of our lives and Jesus, the Word of God, is the rock. So when stuff happens to us, we can remain unshaken.

God reestablishes our broken foundations by giving us identity, revelation, and opportunities to make choices based on hearing His voice! He invites us into a space of understanding, health, and strength to bring us to a place of courage, destiny, breakthrough, and peace in Him! To know the truth about ourselves, about Him, about others, and about our future.

If we want this, we have to lean on His Word and who He says He is. Not who your friends, family, or neighbors say He is, but who He says He is. His Word really does keep us on the right track and correct us when we start to get off. The purpose of knowing God's Word is to establish a foundation in us so that we are equipped in life.

Each day, we get the ability to decide on the destiny and peace we want to walk in. The beauty is, when we make choices with God in mind our decisions are made from a heavenly perspective and give us hope even when things get really tough. Whatever you thought was true about your life before, that narrative didn't develop overnight. So this is a process for all of us: seeing what belongs to the old narrative that passed away, and then strengthening our faith to embrace the much better narrative that God has for all of us.

CHAPTER
seven

{ Discovering
Our Family }

As we build our foundation on the truth of who God says we are, there is one thing that can really expedite our growth. To establish a strong identity that is truly unshakable, we must connect to a family much larger than our individual family unit. We must connect to the family of God, which can give us a greater understanding of what a healthy family can look like. Even better, it can empower us to strengthen our natural families.

Family is a form of community and one of the most important means we have to improve our lives and the lives of those around us. Family gives us values—both good and bad. Family gives us a sense of where we have come from and a springboard to where we will go. It gives us a sense of who we are—good, bad, or ugly. God's original design is for family to provide us with a sense of belonging, nurturing, identity, and love. We are all born desiring these things.

Being connected to God helps us understand what a healthy family looks like. Whether you have an intact family or not, it was intended to help point you to God. Even when family lets us down, we all crave the feeling of love from a community of people that deeply cares about our dreams and hearts. We want others to support our dreams, to believe in us, to love us unconditionally, to give us a sense of value, to express excitement over our potential in life, and to walk alongside us.

God's vision is for all of us to be in His family. He has a vision for family and community that is eternal and that enriches our lives more than any earthly family or community can.

If we don't understand this connection, we automatically start looking for that sense of camaraderie, team, or inclusion elsewhere. We may look to sports, accomplishments, or other things to try to gain this sense of family. Unfortunately, some of those areas are not the most stable or healthy places to pull from.

Anytime there is a void in our lives, our human nature seeks to fill it. I hit a really low place internally; anxiety, depression, and—at times—

thoughts of suicide brushed by my mind and heart. I didn't know what was next, but deep down I believed there had to be something more to life than what I knew. Little did I know it was Some*one*. My emptiness led me to Jesus, and through Jesus to God the Father and the Holy Spirit as Nurturer. Anxiety, depression, and suicide started to lose their grip on my life as I learned how to embrace my journey with God. Those things would try to flare up at times, but my new mindset and heart posture would not allow them to gain any type of foothold in my life. I call it liberty. This same liberty is available to you as well.

Many qualities might come to mind when we think of a healthy family. Without those qualities, we might find ourselves more likely to struggle in some ways in life. The amazing thing about God is that He has a plan even for those who do not have a natural family, or a natural family that models these things well. Jesus came to invite us into His family and relationship with our Father God, which is a gamechanger for all of us! Embracing this truth helps us create a vision for a more grounded life. More importantly, it gives us a sense of hope, especially when things are really dark in our lives.

Family Enjoys Life Together

To feel secure in the family takes time. Just like a plant becomes more grounded as its roots grow deeper, time helps us to become grounded. My mom had to work to put food on our table, so my grandmother gave a lot of her time to help raise me and my sister. I remember walking with her to a place called Thrifty's Ice Cream often.

I remember thinking that was the best thing ever, but reflecting back on it, what I enjoyed most was not the ice cream, but the fact that we were doing something together. My grandmother and I would sit and talk about whatever was on our minds. Sometimes, my sister would come, too, and we would all talk. Those moments left me feeling loved, seen, secure, and connected.

Some of my other favorite childhood memories involve going with my mom to parties at her friend's house. There were always lots of kids there, and spending time with each other and hanging out with one another gave me a sense of community and the connection I craved.

My mom created an atmosphere of fun in our home early on in my childhood, as we spent time with cousins and close family members. We would go to a lot of family friends' houses, too, and hang out with them and their children. When families value connection, just being together is high on their priority list. Whether going to the movies or sitting at home playing board games, families see value in spending time with each other.

Unfortunately, many people who grow up with no father in the home seek this sense of family in all the wrong places. Some fall into gangs, or unhealthy online circles, trying to find some other way of feeling part of something greater than themselves. They're seeking the right thing, but in the wrong way. Now, social media often becomes an artificial substitute for family. This can be inviting but very misleading as well.

Sometimes, people may think they're involved with the right crowds, but then find out that crowd doesn't fill the void. Maybe they are even part of a group that is making a lot of money from someone else's destruction—and then find out that money doesn't fill the void of what true love looks like, either.

I went through a period when I thought I was in the right crowd, too. I started building community with fans and other people who would show up to my games, not people I was living life with day in and day out. I established community in groups of people who didn't have my best interests at heart. These people offered community only if they got something in return. But great community fosters an ecosystem of giving over receiving. In that environment we start to learn that the more we give, the more we start to receive. Early in my career, I was in unhealthy environments that valued "me" over "us," and that impacted my heart, keeping me isolated and misled about what "community" was. I thought, *If I join a gang, maybe I will find what I desire there.* Nope. Then I thought, *If I had a lot of girls, that would give me the status I desire.* Wrong. Or *If I build a big social media following, I would be valued or feel liked.* Way off. What I did inherit, though, were terrible habits from pursuing these things I thought would fill my emptiness. It took years to retrain my mind and heart to know what was valuable and what wasn't.

I was not always the best at family. For example, for a while, I judged people by whether they showed up to my games or not. I also judged others on their passion to hustle. That was the narrow way I defined "family." As I got older, I started to resent my mother for not being able to come to my basketball games. I couldn't understand why they were not her top priority. I didn't have the greatest relationship with her at that time. Little did I know that my attitude was pushing her away. I grew to be ashamed of myself, and I internally projected that shame onto my mother without her even knowing it. I embraced being ashamed of my mom, and it caused a major fracture in our relationship at the time. I was being so selfish and cruel; it took years for me to realize how awful I had become toward someone who truly loved me. Even at times when she may have acted like she didn't love me, deep down she always did, but I was so broken I couldn't see that at all. I failed to realize what she was going through at the time. When our primary focus is "me," we are oblivious to others' situations or hardships. This burdens them even more.

My heart broke when my mom couldn't come to most games—and even when she could, I was still so hurt that I did not want her there. It felt very foreign and odd to me. I felt overwhelming pressure to be extraordinary and make her see that I didn't need her. Part of me felt better knowing she would read or hear about my performance in the game later—like I would have one up on her knowing I had been amazing and she had missed it. I realize now that I made very little effort to spend time showing up for her and doing things that were important to her, or even taking the time to ask if she was all right. It was selfish and dishonoring to have that mentality. Yet, as my heart and mind got rewired with the way, the truth, and the life, my perspective got upgraded. My relationship with my mother got repaired. I was able to rise up from poor mentalities and mishaps that could have destroyed my life. You can also!

God's original design is that we be unified in community, with one another and within our families. He tends to reveal Himself as we walk and grow with one another. He is present as we do life with one another and exhibit what real community looks like. God's dream is for people to see our family and want the same thing. God's version of family extends beyond all biological ties. If we had a traumatic experience with our family, in His grace He will start to repair and rewrite what healthy family looks like, if we let Him.

Proverbs 17:22 says, "A merry heart does good, *like* medicine, but a broken spirit dries the bones." Family is part of God's design for joy in our lives. This can come either with your biological family or a group that is close to you and wants to walk with you as you grow. We mark moments of celebration together, and we get to champion one another. Sometimes, when we grow up in a home where that's not done, we have to become very intentional about it!

Having fun together, celebrating each other, and journeying with one another doesn't necessarily mean things are always going to be quaint and pleasant all the time, but it does mean we can make the effort to enjoy the people around us. When we pursue this mindset, we start to grow stronger and even more grounded in God, and to really offer ourselves a greater chance of having peace in life. More importantly we extend a great invitation for others to choose the same for themselves.

Families Demonstrate Unconditional Love

But God's design for family isn't just to provide support in the good times; I would say that one of God's main values (and the hallmark of a healthy family) is love during our darkest hours. He wants us to follow in His footsteps by spreading love lavishly, without discretion, even in the midst of our circumstances.

Most of us, myself included, have grown up with ideas about love that are conditional. You know—*if you really love me, you would do this for me.* But the love that binds us together is the unconditional love of God. That is the same love God wants us to use with each other.

First Corinthians 13:4-7 defines that love for us. It describes love as "patient" and "kind." It says,

> Love suffers long and is kind; love does not envy; love does not parade itself, is not puffed up; does not behave rudely, does not seek its own, is not provoked, thinks no evil; does not rejoice in iniquity, but rejoices in the truth; bears all things, believes all things, hopes all things, endures all things.

I know that all sounds great. I also know some of you reading this are saying, "But you don't know my story!" I completely understand; it's incredibly hard not to keep any record of wrongs when people have really hurt us! It's hard to be patient at times and often hard to be kind to those who haven't been kind to you. When you succeed, it is hard not to brag in the faces of the people who said you'd never amount to anything and say, "Look at that! You were wrong, and I was right!"

It's hard as well not to be self-seeking. Our culture teaches us the opposite. It teaches you to get yours, hustle all day, disregard others in your pursuit of success, get in where you fit in, and make yourself the greatest. But those things can potentially drive wedges in our relationships and separate us from our family and genuine connection with people. Those connections are quickly becoming lost in our society.

Part of unconditional love is accepting that others will fail us, disappoint us, and make mistakes—but that doesn't have to curtail our love for each other. We have to know that we can't find perfect love in imperfect people. The only perfect love obtainable is the love of God, and the only way we can be separated from that is if by our choice, because He never turns His love off toward us. The Apostle Paul writes in Romans 8:38-39:

> For I am persuaded that neither death nor life, nor angels nor principalities nor powers, nor things present nor things to come, nor height nor depth, nor any other created thing, shall be able to separate us from the love of God which is in Christ Jesus our Lord.

There will be times when our families go through very tough seasons. Times when failure comes into the picture. However, God's desire for us is not to give up on each other, but to grow in deep, affectionate love for one another. Many times, our darkest moments can help us grow into deeper love. Or maybe you know someone who just drives you crazy!!! I heard that people who anger you the most help to perfect love in you the most deeply. That love can only be realized when we understand God's love for us and our families.

God's family does not abuse, shame, control, or intimidate to "punish" each other for mistakes. When you make a mistake as part of God's family, you should be able to apologize and say you're sorry without feeling like you're weak or compromising your stance. Being emotionally vulnerable with your family shows that you are human as well. It also shows that you are willing to grow into a new level of maturity. This level often requires us to extend humility and grace even when we are 100 percent right and the other person is completely out of line!

Another hallmark of a healthy family is that people communicate with truth and grace and open their hearts to listen to the other person without offense. They feel safe to communicate their thoughts, concerns, and needs. They communicate when they are hurt so that the issue can be resolved; they look for ways to resolve things. We love each other well when we share our perspective and ideas. Ephesians 4:14–15 says that by "speaking the truth in love, we may grow up in all things into Him who is the head—Christ…"

None of this can actually happen if we are not spending time with each other. People make mistakes and situations can get messy. Sometimes people think they love someone, but actually, they don't spend enough time with that person to demonstrate the kind of love that forgives, that covers mistakes, that is selfless. Jesus came to spend time demonstrating His love for us, and it takes time for a family to demonstrate love as well.

Family Gives Us Values

Good family values, in big and small ways, reflect God. Jesus had a clear set of values, starting with valuing people more than anything. He also demonstrated the importance of passing values on to other generations. I think one of the primary roles of a parent (after being willing to spend time with your child and loving him or her unconditionally) is that you want to instill great character, strong core values, a flexible heart and mind that is willing to listen—values that are deeply planted and which help direct and establish peace, purpose, and hope. All those values should point our children toward their destiny of helping others to do the same.

For example, my mom taught me the value of relationships and what it means to know different people. If you were to ask people who know me now, they would say my value for relationships is probably one of my greatest attributes. I'm able to connect fairly easily with people. I value relationships with others because it gives me greater capacity to model healthy connection to the world.

My mom was always telling me how important it is to really take time to know people and talk to them. Not only that, but she would model it as I was watching. My mom wasn't even a Christian at the time. She didn't have a relationship with the Lord but she knew those things were good, and I knew they were good. Now I know that is because God is good, and we are attracted to things that are of Him. We have His DNA.

For example, Jesus would take time to sit with people and talk to them; they would have life-changing encounters just by Him simply being human to them. In John 3, Jesus met with a religious leader of the region. His name was Nicodemus, and he was curious about what Jesus was teaching about the way to the Kingdom of God, and if what he was doing was wrong. He had many questions, and he was humbling himself to seek to understand more about faith, even though he was a top religious leader. He sought greater understanding of that to which he had dedicated his life. He also wanted to know if there was hope for him as a religious leader, teacher, and influencer amongst people? The Lord took the time to speak to Nicodemus in the middle of the night, and from there we see a transformation start to take place in Nicodemus's heart and mind.

Another time, Jesus spoke with a woman at a well in Samaria. It was against culture, tradition, and law for a Jewish man to speak to a Samaritan woman alone—but He did, and in doing so redeemed her and modeled to His followers how to bring hope and resurrection to others when they are dying inside.

Even though our relationship was rocky when I was young, I learned from my mother the importance of seeing people, talking to them, and having authentic relationships with them. I can say now one of the greatest treasures my mom has ever given me was understanding how to be in authentic relationship with others.

My mom also instilled in me some other core values as well. She was a "get it done at any cost" type of mom. She ingrained in me a value for productivity—"Don't be lazy, don't rely on someone else to provide for you." "Be willing to go out and work hard on your own and don't ever take no as an answer." "There's always a way; even if you have to be more creative, you can figure out a way to continually work hard." "Be willing to put the time into what you believe is going to be something worth pursuing." This was invaluable to me. It propelled me into playing basketball, pursuing my dreams, and exploring what it looks like to work hard at anything you desire to do.

Finally, she demonstrated to me the importance of really honoring your parents, which many times I failed to do. She showed me it was important to spend time with family. I know this was tough for her, as her own parents didn't have much of a relationship and had not modeled this to her when she was a child. Yet, she still did her best to instill this value in me out of her pain and past experience.

Family Nurtures Your Dreams

I'll never forget the day I came home to find that my mom had put up a basketball hoop right in the little courtyard on the side of our apartment building. It wasn't very big, but it had enough space for me to dribble and play ball. I started having friends come over and we'd be dunking on that rim! We had fun. I was out there all the time, dribbling the ball day in, day out, day in, day out. I'm sure my neighbors hated that, but it gave me the chance to really explore the dream God had put in my heart all the way back then.

I just remember that as one of the most loving things my mom ever did for me. She noticed how much I loved to play basketball and how much I idolized Michael Jordan when I was a young kid. So she did what she could to provide that environment for me. She would allow me to walk to the park from my house (which is unheard of nowadays, but it was safe back then). That was another place where I played and practiced my skills.

She demonstrated a belief in my dreams even with her limited resources. She believed in me—but I had to get active in order to fulfill the dreams in my heart, and overcome the barriers and roadblocks. Even though I'm blessed enough to be able to provide for my kids, there are still times we have to be creative and find solutions other than just what is given to us. The church where I pastor and the families I meet with have to innovate at times as well. In that innovation, we can discover strong solutions.

In order to empower each other to fulfill our dreams, however, we have to notice each other and our unique skills, gifts, and callings. God would also have us affirm the value and uniqueness of others as a way to demonstrate love. Romans 15:7 says, "Therefore receive one another, just as Christ also received us, to the glory of God."

I have three children and they all have different passions, different desires, different likes and dislikes. They are different, so I have to speak to them and nurture them differently. They all have the same foundation in Christ, but they all receive it differently. Accepting them and working to understand them and their dreams is what family is meant to do. It's also a journey we go on as we grow as a unit.

I may not have had strong examples of relationship with the Lord when I was growing up, but I still have the reward of being able to instill in my children core values that will establish our family on a firm foundation in future generations.

Family Shows You Better Options by Modeling
We can learn a lot about family by observing successful characteristics in others. When I met my wife and started to spend time with her family, I was shocked by how they operated. They would get into full-blown arguments with each other, but ten seconds later they would make up and be friends again. My family was not like that; my family held grudges. So her family baffled me.

I would say, "You should be upset, and you should stay upset."

My wife's family dynamic was the opposite of mine, which was a healthier model for disagreement. It was like, "Hey, get your grievances out. We still love each other. We still care for each other. Let's move forward." When I married my wife, this was an area where I had to realize I was not strong. After I met Christ this came to light even more. I had to learn how to communicate in truth and grace, how to affirm uniqueness, how to not intimidate my wife, and continually build our spiritual foundation and respect for one another. I also had to learn that conflict resolution was one of my weakest areas. This dramatically impacted my relationships with people, primarily my family.

When I gave my life to God, those were all things I had to begin reconstructing in my mind and my heart. Obviously, it's an ongoing process. No one has figured it all out. All of us are looking for examples of how to do this well, consciously or unconsciously, in different places. Growing up, I would watch TV shows with fictional families and think to myself, "They have it all together." I would try to model the good or reenact what I saw on TV to no avail.

My desire for role models at that time was very slight—especially male role models. As a young boy in the minority community, there wasn't much for me to gravitate toward. This void in my life left me feeling hopeless and at times confused about what healthy direction looked like. I didn't find real-life modeling for it until I discovered relationship with God—then it impacted me and my wife together. We started to discover what healthy relationship was, which helped us to model that to our own family. The most amazing part was that it transformed each of our families.

Not having a parental figure in the house, or being fatherless, really impacts us. Sometimes we end up feeling lost within our own families. One day, a Superior Court judge told me that more than 90 percent of the young people he had to sentence grew up with no parental guidance in the home. Of those, 75 percent did not have fathers in their lives. Most of the young people who were making mistakes were making them from a lack of guidance in their lives, not because they wanted to commit crimes. They just were not taught right from wrong at home, so they learned it from people who did not model it appropriately (gangs, movies, friends, etc.). This inevitably landed them in situations where they had to pay with their lives for their misled decisions. It was heartbreaking.

Maybe you're not getting the love, teaching, or modeling you desire at home. Maybe your family members aren't coming around and you feel isolated. This is one reason God wants us in His family—so that we are never without a good model or left feeling like orphans. God says in John 14:18, "I will not leave you orphans; I will come to you." That's a statement filled with hope, and that hope is available for anyone reading this right now. That's the hope that saved my life, and I know it can do the same for you.

I had to discover and establish many things about family later in life. The only way I was able to discover them was through my relationship with my Heavenly Father. Even though I didn't have an earthly father, my Heavenly Father started to demonstrate being a father to me by providing the things I lacked; by bringing me comfort, confidence, and courage to grow in areas that were empty. He also started to show me the things that He was going to replenish in my heart so that there wouldn't be a void anymore. I believe He will do the same thing for you if you want that for your life.

When you become a follower of Christ, the Word of God will actively cultivate your heart and stir you to do things that bring change and growth in your life. The Word of God is modeling to you from the inside out, so you are lacking nothing, according to James 1:4. Psalm 119:105 says that His Word is a lamp to our feet and a light to our paths. Philippians 1:6 says "that He who has begun a good work in you will complete *it* until the day of Jesus Christ." This tells me that good work has already begun in me. But that good work is only as powerful and clear as my revelation of God. So, I can study and spend time with God in order to have clearer revelation.

Our natural families can provide us with good modeling, but even then, we need God's strength, perspective, and a lot of time to walk in it. I don't believe we will arrive overnight. Obviously, those whose parents have modeled good relationship and conflict resolution tend to pick it up a whole lot faster, but they still need the support of an ever-present Father to help. Everything changes when we recognize that the eternal God is our Father here on Earth as well. When we understand this, we start to access what we need in terms of time and attention, unconditional love, resources, and modeling. The invitation is for all of us. The question is, do we want to receive it? Do YOU want to receive it?

Family Points Us to God's Original Design

Before mothers and fathers existed, God was a Parent. What are some of His parenting traits? Many think of mothers in general as demonstrating consistency, commitment, and steadfastness. Mothers teach us how to love our family, how to nurture, and how to stay connected emotionally.

Mothers often have to serve as protectors, nurturers, and providers. Mothers are fiercely loyal to their children. They work hard, they are intuitive, they are creative, they create solutions when there aren't any solutions. Mothers often have inner strength or faith. There are a lot of praying mothers who are on their knees daily, wanting the best life for their children. Even when the odds are stacked against them, mothers often find creative ways—some good and some not—to provide. Most single-parent homes are led by mothers, and that means they have to play the role of both parents. That is a monumental task.

Men often feel their role as a father is reduced to just being a provider, but that lie needs to be completely torn down. As a father, you have to be the most willing to put your family in a position to receive all that God has for them. You create and foster the environment they grow in. Fathers also have the opportunity to teach their children how to respect and protect others, how to think through things, and how to give and seek wise counsel. Being a father means spending time, having deep conversations, laughing at jokes, and reflecting who THE Father is to your family. He's patient, He's kind, He's good, He's faithful. Mothers also have the ability to do these things, but as a father, it's one of your greatest privileges to model to children the core values to build their lives upon.

The beauty of this is that anyone, whether they know God or not, can observe and embody great things to the next generation. If you have not seen these things in your life, God is the perfect Person to demonstrate them to you, so you are not lacking anything.

Jesus As a Model of Hope

In Luke 2, Jesus is twelve years old and His parents are leaving Jerusalem, where they had gone for Passover. But Jesus stays behind, and His parents don't realize it because there is a whole caravan of people walking back to Nazareth together. They are all doing life together—so much so that the parents are confident that the rest of the caravan family is keeping an eye on Jesus.

Obviously, He isn't with them. And when they realize it, they went go to Jerusalem and spend three days looking for Him. So can you imagine the hysteria and panic. Losing a child is one of the worst things a parent can go through. It turns out that Jesus is in the Temple courts among teachers. He is sitting with them, asking questions and teaching. The Bible says His parents saw that and were astonished. They said, "Why have you treated us like this, son?" He replied, "You didn't know I needed to be in My father's house?"

So what does that tell us? It tells us that your family can love you, but sometimes they're not tracking with you. But that doesn't mean you're not right where you need to be with God's family. Jesus was in His Heavenly Father's house, teaching and asking questions.

Jesus was right where He needed to be. That is something we can learn from: Even when others think we should be lost in our family situation or our community, we don't have to stay lost. We can be right where we need to be with the Father—in His house, in His presence, in prayer with Him, being one with Him. And when people finally discover that you aren't lost, they will be astonished. Even if you seem lost to others, you are completely found in Him.

The passage says that Jesus grew in wisdom and in stature and in favor with God and man. In order for us to grow in wisdom and His stature, but more importantly in faith, we can't allow our past to dictate our future. God has already paid the price for those things. We need to be in our Father's house. We need to be one with Him. We need to be in relationship with Him. In doing so, we can have peace in storms as well as in success. This is something we can learn and pass down to our children.

So when we talk about healthy family processes, one is to be one with God and that we would be family with one another in community. But even when we get lost within our communities, as long as we're in the Father's house, we'll be easy to find. We can feel at home and be at peace.

What is the big invitation for us in this? It is to invite God in and fix our perspective, our identity, and even our past. There's hope for a sense of family in our lives. Even in our worst circumstances, we can have peace and the promise that things can be greater in our lives. You are invited to understand who God is as your Father.

Living in a fatherless home brought a lot of questions. It did not ultimately define me, because it also allowed me to really go on a journey of finding out what the love of Father God looks like. My past, although painful at times, gave me some wonderful opportunities in basketball. I didn't understand then that God was grooming me to coach on a grander level, which is coaching people's lives. Sharing the hope of Glory and the love of God with them, the core values of healthy living.

Nothing is lost with God. No matter your family situation, He has redemption in mind, and He can bring that redemption to you if you allow Him.

God's Idea of Family, Mirrored in the Church

There is a reason that we are known as members of God's family after accepting Jesus (Ephesians 2:19). We are to be an example of His family—not just to our immediate family, but to our world! We are to model values to others, as well as nurture their God-given dreams and destinies, demonstrate unconditional love, and spend time together.

God's original design for the family is beautiful. Psalm 133:1 says, "Behold, how good and how pleasant *it is* for brethren to dwell together in unity!" That unity is exactly what God desires for us to have—that we be one as Jesus, the Spirit, and the Father are one, and that it would stem from the home and family.

God's original intent was for us to be unified and to do life with one another. This helps us to become grounded in our identity as part of the family of God. We see this in the way the disciples became unified in their journey together, the persecution they went through, the signs and miracles, and walking with Jesus together. When times were hard, they would strengthen and encourage one another. I believe that is what family really looks like. When you're really family, things can get tough. But God's design is for us to be together as one unit in the midst of both hard and joyous times.

As we do this, we start to reflect God's light to other people. The world around us starts to notice, and that brings glory to God. As Proverbs 22:6 tells us that if you start a child off the way he should go, even when he is old, he won't turn from it. But in order to start someone else off in the right direction, we first need to do it ourselves. We then need to be available for them as we help them down that path. Helping others is one of the greatest privileges we have in this life.

CHAPTER
eight

{ Belonging }

Most of us spend a lot of time and energy trying to belong in life. One of the biggest lessons I have learned is: to truly belong, you have to serve those around you. You don't fully achieve a sense of belonging in life until you give things away. This is where the reward of feeling grounded starts to increase exponentially for us.

Knowing we have something to offer gives us a powerful sense of meaning, value, and purpose. Serving our community is essential to gaining self-esteem, confidence, and identity. Sadly, it's often overlooked and unrecognized. I think we tend not to grasp the impact of serving our community because in our American culture, it's all about providing for yourself and getting ahead personally.

Community is not always highly valued. Our culture teaches us to work for individual goals and victories, but the Kingdom of God is the opposite: if you learn how to serve people, you become the greatest in life. That greatness is experienced through very rich relationships, and people that will help you feel seen, known, heard, and champion you because you modeled it to them first.

I believe community is very important to God. God Himself does not live in isolation. He is the Father, Son, and Holy Spirit. They're all in sync with one another and they're all talking and ministering to each other and to us. And yet, God is described as three in one, and we see Him describe Himself as one being made of several others. He is a community.

When you serve others, there will be seasons for you to get ahead, and people will want to invest in helping you because you invested in them first. I think a healthy community has multiple layers, which is why I keep talking about it throughout this book. We are stronger in community than we are apart. We see that in sports teams: not one person can play all the positions, so we need each person to show up and contribute what they have in order to win. We know where we belong. Even in individual sports, there is always a strong committed team behind the athlete competing.

Barriers to Knowing the Power of Serving

Sometimes, there are practical barriers to discovering the power of serving, especially when we have grown up without resources or in unhealthy environments. Maybe we can't get around a healthy community where we see it is natural for people to serve or help each other. Maybe this is because a parent has to work, or others can't drive us to church, etc. Sometimes we end up making up a community in our mind based on TV, social media, or music. In our minds, people serve us, so when we get into the real world, we're not sure what we have to give, or why we should give it.

Parents play a huge role in establishing a healthy community for their children to discover their identity and purpose for life. The first community you are introduced to is your family. It is hard to help children learn to serve the household when it's easier and takes less time for the adult to do the chores themselves. When a father is not present in the family, the chances of a child stumbling into bad environments and trying to create belonging in unhealthy ways increases.

When there isn't an adult helping you intentionally create your community, it is hard to find one organically. You're more apt to find unhealthy communities as opposed to healthy ones, because healthy communities require full engagement. When we are young, especially, there are so many things we don't know and can't do to remove barriers to being in these communities.

I think young people from single-parent homes are most likely to find belonging in unhealthy communities just because there are not enough resources. They don't have someone to champion them. We all want some kind of community, and unhealthy ones embrace us with a synthetic love and a feeling of belonging, but bring with them unhealthy values.

That's what a lot of gang life tends to be. Gangs make you feel like you're a part of something. It's very tribal in nature. Everyone needs attention in life and to feel that they matter, and gangs will give you attention for doing things that line up with their values—even if those things are destructive. Whatever your dreams are, none of these unhealthy communities will cultivate them in healthy ways. More importantly, your dreams can quickly turn into nightmares when they are cultivated in the wrong context.

I remember being on a school bus when I was young and watching kids teasing each other. They'd be cracking jokes and making fun of each other (we called it capping or clowning). If you couldn't hold your own on that bus, you would get torn apart and tormented daily. If you were actually really good at making fun of people, you were revered as someone with authority and influence. So I became really good at being the guy who made fun of people.

I was accepted because I had a great sense of humor. That was a form of belonging to me, even though it came at the expense of tearing someone else down. The idea that I belonged because I made fun of people was a lie from the pit of Hell. That was how desperate I was to be valued. That's how desperate I was to feel embraced by my friends.

There were also times within my basketball community when some of the guys didn't accept me. That hurt me because I felt like I was doing the same thing they were doing, and they still rejected me. That seed of rejection was planted in my heart long before I started playing sports, and it would flare up at times. My root of rejection was always an underlying feeling that would show its ugly head when those I wanted to embrace me pushed me away.

Even as an adult, when someone didn't receive me or want me to be around them, I would get offended. I just wanted to be liked and loved. If I thought you liked me, I felt I belonged. This is why so many people get led into the wrong communities: they are just looking for someone to like them and accept them—and humans will compromise a lot to be liked and accepted. They will even do things that are out of their character to feel like they belong.

It's really difficult to get to that sense of sustained belonging without God. It's even tougher to understand service to others when you have that void. When you feel you have to put on a front and be someone else to be accepted, you are always afraid of losing that acceptance. You will feel like you cannot make mistakes and you are often afraid you will be judged.

The risk is that you will start to put up a facade and become phony—internally first, and then externally, sometimes knowingly, sometimes not. And then when you do get into a healthy environment, you don't even recognize it. You've created this whole synthetic montage of your life that prevents you from understanding what being known looks like.

We Belong When We Serve

When I played professional basketball in other countries, my contract stipulated that I had to go out and serve the community for a certain number of hours every week. Giving back was nonnegotiable. So during that time, I often helped with basketball camps for inner-city kids.

Professional basketball brings a lot of stress and pressure. I felt like there was extra pressure on me because I was American and had been brought overseas as "the expert"; I was the highest-paid person on the team. There was a lot of expectation on me at all times.

What I soon realized was that getting a chance to go out and just be with young kids and the community relieved me from that pressure for a time. It felt great to get out and engage with people. This mindset is just one of the reasons community service is good for us in general.

When I was playing in England, I used to go help at a school for inner-city kids who were not on a good path in life. Many times, after playing a game, we would sit down and talk about things that were not even related to basketball. I would just give them an opportunity to ask questions and express how they felt.

A lot of them would ask about the music I liked, or other normal, everyday things. I remember this one kid asked me how I dealt with being away from home and if I had ever argued with my parents when I was growing up. I thought, "Wow, I can't believe a kid this age would ask me something like that."

That opened up questions from all the other forty kids in the group. It took one kid being brave enough to ask that type of vulnerable question to give courage to the other kids. I was more blessed by that question than they were by my answer. This is another reason why service is so important: often, we find ourselves feeling more blessed and fulfilled when we serve others with no agenda attached.

I felt blessed because I didn't even ask the question or try to open up the kids' hearts; I was just there for them and with them in that moment. I saw what it did for those kids to be free and comfortable enough to ask, feeling they weren't going to be judged. They weren't going to be laughed at. Granted, I was American, and they knew they were not going to interact with me every single day, but I think they felt that day like they belonged.

As they started to open up, I realized most of them had childhoods very similar to my own. They felt rejected, they were trying to belong, they didn't have very much guidance, and they ended up committing crimes out of desperation—sometimes to feel accepted. When we are open to serving others, we recognize that we are not alone, and we may be more alike than we think.

I would often ask those kids, "What do you want to do with your life?" And 95 percent of them would say, "I just want to live and not die." It was one of the most heartbreaking things to hear a young kid say. Almost none of them had fathers in their homes, but most of them were desiring direction and belonging. All of them wanted to feel valued.

The next week, when I went back to do the camp, the group had doubled! We had twice as many kids as before because they felt like they could come to this camp and not feel shamed or ridiculed. Instead, they felt valued and seen.

When I saw the camp doubled that next week, I felt really blessed and humbled. I thought, "Are you going to take the time to spend with kids and give them really sound and honest advice that would help them?" I felt like what I was bringing meant something to them—something they wanted to tell their friends about. I felt fulfillment wrapped in love for one of the very first times I can remember.

Service prepares us. Pretty much every career, at its core, is about serving someone in some way. Whether a boss, company, or customer, we are meant to serve each other. Little did I know pro basketball was God's way of preparing me for what I was going to be doing down the line when I became a high school head coach, working with young athletes, then serving political leaders, and now pastoring. I basically went from coaching student athletes to coaching all kinds of people in their identities.

I'm coaching on a grander scale now. It's like God was preparing me from the very beginning to do this, and I didn't even have a relationship with Him. At the time, I didn't have any type of understanding of who God was.

What I found was my real purpose in this life is to be completely in agreement with what God called me to do. Community service helps shape your identity because you start to see the goodness of God when you're able to give back to others without seeking anything in return. I call that a "deposit mindset" over a "withdrawal mindset"—and it's exactly the kind that God has for us.

You Belong When You Know God Made You

Remember my church experience when I was trying to impress that girl in high school? I did not go to church for myself; it was to impress her. I felt a lie from the enemy saying that I already failed; I was having sex in high school, and I wasn't good enough. I thought my sin disqualified me.

Sometimes people come to church who don't necessarily speak the lingo or feel like they fit in. It's like putting on a suit when you've worn shorts, T-shirts, and flip-flops your entire life. You just feel totally uncomfortable and out of place. It makes it uncomfortable. It is hard to deal with that discomfort without God's help.

My biggest breakthrough came when I realized I belong because He says I belong, not because I perform well or because others like me. When that happens, you carry your belonging into other situations and start helping others feel they belong, too. When you allow yourself to be stretched in that area and wear the tailored suit, so to speak, you are able to go into different spheres of influence with different kinds of people.

There's no greater validation than when God says you belong to Him. We're made to seek that belonging because we're made in His image. So when He says that we are His, there's no greater validation. You are made in His image and He put you in this world to reflect that original design.

After I gave my life to the Lord, He started opening up great opportunities for me to be around profound circles of people—very influential, very diverse people. When you start running with influential athletes, politicians, and businesspeople, you can start to think you've become a success because they have embraced you when the truth of the matter is, God has given you the opportunity to influence them with the core values He has instilled in you.

I constantly have to ask God to check my heart in this area. I don't have these opportunities solely because those people have embraced me; it's because God has embraced me first. And when God embraces you, He opens doors and allows you to be in those circles so that you will reflect Him into them—not by what you're preaching, but by how you're living your life.

Also, when you get thrust into these circles, they won't change you. They won't persuade you to start acting in a different way, because your sense of belonging doesn't come from them. Your sense of validation and belonging starts with God. They will be a guide to you and an external representation of what God is like to them.

The Importance of Encouraging Others

Even though others' words can hold us back or even derail us in life, encouraging words have the ability to empower us. I believe God has called us all to be encouragers; this is one way we can help change the world.

Now, I am not saying to encourage unrealistic fantasies, but to bring some cheerleading to people in our lives and say, "Hey, you can do this and if you believe in yourself, we believe in you." Even the best athletes perform better when they can feed off the cheers of others; we are all the same in that way. A little encouragement can give us energy and hope to do our best. Encouragement is one of the greatest gifts we have been entrusted with. It's also one of the greatest ways we have to help others feel empowered.

We see this in the Bible in the story of how Saul became the Apostle Paul. Saul was not a good person. In fact, he was an enemy of the Church. Most believers probably would have said that Saul would never amount to anything good—he was killing Christians at the time!

But there was a man named Barnabas. The Bible calls him "the son of encouragement." When Saul met Jesus and became known as Paul, Barnabas was the one who introduced him to all the Christians and vouched for him. He essentially said, "Hey, this guy was killing Christians a little while ago, but now he is lined up with God's vision and identity for himself now. Now he's OK. He's a follower of Christ." Barnabas's words carried weight with the other Christians. He was a person of encouragement, and he no doubt encouraged Paul as well, helping him lean into and start to really partner with the identity God had for him.

Paul went on to write twelve books of the New Testament and to pen the words that encourage and empower so many Christians to this day! When Barnabas and Paul later split up to do ministry in different places, Barnabas took a man named Mark with him; Mark also later wrote a book of the Bible.

Most people do not think about Barnabas, but his encouraging words helped lay the foundation for others to write almost half of the New Testament in the bible. CRAZY!!!

So, encouragement is very powerful. It is a gift God gave us to create change in ourselves, in others, and in our world. When we encourage one person, the ripple effect goes beyond them to change our whole community for good!

You Belong When You Simply Bring What You Have
Some people think they have to have or be something special in order to serve. Nothing is further from the truth! We can all benefit from serving others. I believe the best role models are not the ones who are the greatest, the smartest, or the best at something. The best role models are simply the ones who want to help, to make a difference, and who are available! In my little basketball community growing up, there was a guy named Windale who would take me to the basketball court, allow me to play and make mistakes, and grow.

Being with him was profound because he didn't judge me. He championed me. He believed in me. He was my role model for those reasons. People like Windale may or may not know God, but they believe in us. They may see something in us, or they may be trying to get something from us, but they become role models simply by paying attention to us, these role models offer us the courage to dream and hope for greater in our lives.

I first started getting to know God during my last year of playing professional basketball, when one of my teammates wanted to start a charity foundation in his home country of Nigeria. He had been working on it for about two years, but there was still no money involved, no sponsorship or anything like that.

My teammate asked if I would visit in the summer and teach kids how to play basketball. I had never been to Africa and I felt God saying I needed to go. So I said, "Hey, you know, I would love to come as long as I get the opportunity to preach the Gospel of Jesus Christ." I didn't even think of myself as having a strong relationship with God at the time; I just believed in Him and that He had a plan for my life.

My teammate said I could come preach whatever I liked as long as I taught basketball. I said, "Great."

Fast forward: That year, things didn't go too well in my life and my basketball career was coming to an end. But after I left the team, I gave my life to Christ wholeheartedly while listening to an online church service at work one night.

I still felt the Lord saying, "Yes, you need to go to Africa." So later that summer, I did. I didn't know anything about anything; I had just given my life to the Lord. I wasn't a seasoned teacher or preacher. I thought I would start collecting Bibles to give away, so I started emailing a lot of organizations, asking them to send me Bibles.

One group in Oregon that collected old Bibles said, "Why don't you just become a drop point for all of these old Bibles that come in? We can't take them anymore."

I said, "Great! You send them to me!" And right before I left for Africa, I got three boxes full of Bibles.

I packed one big hockey bag full of Bibles and another full of basketballs, put my clothes in one carry-on, and flew to Nigeria. My heart just wanted to preach the Gospel. When I landed in Nigeria, airport security pulled me aside and took me into an interrogation room.

It was me and a lot of customs officials and security guards. I was really nervous because I had never been to Africa before. The security guards were walking around with AK-47 assault rifles. There was security EVERYWHERE, and they all had guns!

As I was sitting there, they told me to get up and unzip a bag. So I unzipped the bag of basketballs and thought, "Whew, that's OK." Then they told me to unzip the other bag, and I got really scared because I didn't know what was going on. I also didn't know if bringing in Bibles was even legal. But I unzipped the bag full of Bibles and one of the officials looked at me and said, "You know those are Bibles, don't you?"

I said yes, thinking, *Oh man, I'm about to be thrown in jail.* And he said again, "Those are Bibles."

Again I said, "Yeah."

He said, "Why do you have Bibles?"

I said, "Because I'm going to preach the Gospel of Christ to kids at a basketball camp."

"Oh, you're going to teach basketball here?" he asked

"Yes.

"You're going to talk about Jesus?"

I said, "Yes."

The official left the room, and I found myself thinking , *Oh man, I'm gonna get in more trouble.*

He came back in and said, "OK, you're free to go on one condition: can I have a Bible for me and all my friends that are here right now?"

I was like, *Oh my God, yes, absolutely!*

06.18.2010

So I gave him some Bibles and we took pictures. I prayed for them before I left. I was in total shock because I thought I was going to jail, and I thought that guy was going to ridicule me for my faith—or worse. But it turned out to be the opposite. It was like something straight out of the Bible—like God opening the door for me to move on.

I get emotional even thinking about it now, but the story doesn't end there. I went to the camp and was teaching basketball. I knew I was about to start giving out the Bibles on a certain night. When the time came, I looked in the bag and said, "OK, kids, if any of you want a Bible, line up right here. I'm going to give you guys Bibles."

I did not expect all six hundred kids in the camp to line up to get a Bible. I knew I didn't have six hundred Bibles in my hockey bag; it wasn't even big enough to fit six hundred Bibles! Not only that, you also can't even put six hundred Bibles on a plane because that is seriously heavy and you gotta pay extra money for that to be shipped.

So I was looking at my bag thinking, *Oh man, these kids all want Bibles. I'm not going to be able to get more Bibles.* But I started handing them out, thinking maybe I'd just get the information from the kids at the end of the line and ship some over later. So I kept passing out Bibles, passing out Bibles, passing out Bibles, and the line was *long*. And then I started noticing the line getting shorter, but everyone was still getting a Bible. I kept looking at my bag and thinking, *How is this happening?* Still I kept passing them out and passing them out.

Finally, the line ended and every kid had received a Bible. I looked in my bag and found I actually had Bibles left over. God multiplied His Word right in front of my very eyes. And He did it in front of all of the other camp counselors as well.

The next day, I told my teammate who started the foundation that I wanted to have a church service on Sunday. So we did, and I

preached the Gospel. A lot of the kids ended up giving their lives to Jesus, including some who were Muslim. That is a *very* dramatic decision, because in their culture, accepting Jesus can cost a person his life.

I preached about Jesus and baptized about thirty kids, as well as six coaches. A lot of them were saying, "This is the best camp we've ever had, not because of the basketballs, but because the Gospel of Jesus Christ was being preached." I thought, *Wow, I can do this all my living days, preach the Gospel and reach people in a community.* Serving made me feel alive, like I was noticed and appreciated. I had a purpose. I belonged because I was grafted into the Body of Christ. Also there was no pressure on me to be an expert—all I had to do was point people toward the Way, the Truth, and the Life.

The story doesn't end there, though! I later helped many of the kids from that camp come to America. They all went to Christian high schools, and most of them ended up going to college. A lot of them got married and started families. Some of them have gone back to Nigeria to help their country grow and do the same thing I did.

So when we talk about the importance of community service, you have to remember you don't know who you're impacting. God multiplies your efforts and service, especially if they come from selfless motives. You don't have to be qualified in some big way. I had just become a Christian when this happened; I didn't know anything, but I went with the intention of just blessing, serving, and helping others the best I knew how, and to declare the goodness of God over those schools, those kids, and that country and region. I ended up going back four more times, and saw many young kids and adults give their lives to the Lord. But it all started out by serving another person's vision, and then serving a community and getting involved.

This is God's vision for our lives: that we know we are His and made in His image. From that place, we imitate Christ in how we serve the people around us. That gives us a great way to see the way, the truth, and the life manifest before our very eyes.

CHAPTER

nine

{
Crossroads:
Keys for Making
Life-Altering
Decisions
}

When I was cut from the last professional basketball team I played for, I flew back home. My athletic career was over. I was getting older, and I just didn't have the passion and desire to continue to play anymore. I didn't like the up and down of it, and quite frankly, I was ready for something greater.

However, those realizations brought me to one of my lowest points in life, because I didn't know what was next. I was at a crossroad. I wasn't sure which was the right way to go. I was just like, "Man, this sucks, I don't know what to do." So I did all I knew how to do, which was go back to my job as the overnight security at the golf resort where I started.

However, once I committed my heart to Jesus, I needed a whole new model for how to live and how to make good decisions on a consistent basis. I wanted to make decisions that would bring my life consistently closer to the way, the truth, and the life that God had for me.

I was tested in this when I got the opportunity to move back to San Diego, where I had been born and raised, and work at a church. As you know, I didn't grow up in church, so I didn't know anything about having a "ministry" or even what that meant. I just knew that environment gave me the best opportunity to grow as a husband and as a follower of Jesus. It also was a place for me to understand how to help others fulfill their destiny in life as well.

It was not an easy decision. My wife wasn't a Christian at the time, and we had just had our third child. I got so much pushback from both my family and my in-laws because they didn't understand. They were like, "Oh man, you're going to be a preacher?! You're going to go after God?!" I knew I was uprooting my family to pursue something I had no background in, but I felt that was where I was supposed to go.

I only knew I had to stay focused on the promise that God had given me. The distractions of Hell in your life have no power against the promises of Heaven for your life. And since I had been on this journey with God, I had started to develop a filter and processes for making decisions for myself and my family. This has helped me tremendously, and I hope creating a process like this will help you, also.

The first question I ask about any decision I have to make is: Does this glorify God? Deep in my spirit and in my heart, do I feel a desire to do something that is right and honoring to God? And even if I don't know that answer, would I be willing to step out in faith to try to do so?

Second: Would I be willing and proud to impart or teach this to my children? Would I be proud to see them do this?

Third: Will this help me be a better person for my family?

And finally: Will this choice enable me to serve and be a blessing to other people around me?

Those things have been some of my decision-making measurables. When I make decisions based on those questions, it doesn't mean that I don't get pushback. In moving to San Diego to work at a church, I certainly did get pushback, but it gave me an opportunity to identify some different measurables in my decision-making process. It also gave me assurance in pursuing something different for my life.

I felt comfortable passing it on to my children, as well as other people around me and their families. It would be something that would go on from generation to generation to generation.

But it was a hard decision to make. Growing up without a father in the home had really stripped me of my confidence to do things and to dream big. I didn't have much confidence or experience in making life-changing decisions, either. I struggled a lot with the fear that it would blow up in my face. That I would always have to feel ashamed or like a failure. That there would be no one to catch me if I messed up and pick me up again. Or more importantly, no one to help me rise up, dust myself off, and keep going. I had all these lies in my head saying that I would not be a success. It was so strongly ingrained in my DNA of thinking.

The crazy part is that there actually is success in failures. There is success in taking leaps of faith. You're gonna fall flat on your face sometimes. You're gonna fall on your back. But when you have faith and hope and you really root your heart in the promises of God, when you do fall on your face it is not going to derail you. It's not going to get your life-long attention. It's not going to consume the entirety of your walk of life, because there is an abounding love covering you. That's when we discover that life is not about us; it's about glorifying God and helping others. In focusing on those principles we discover true value and abundant purpose.

Psalms 86:5 says, "For You, Lord, *are* good, and ready to forgive, and abundant in mercy to all those who call upon You." In my journey, I was calling to God about these things. The biggest, scariest leap for me was moving to San Diego and going into full-time service to God in the church. I didn't know what I was doing. I had no background in that, and I felt like I was going into an environment that was held to the highest standard. There was no room for failure.

But I started to realize that when we use this decision-making process, we are not fully responsible for making the outcome happen the way the world thinks it should. Our success in the Kingdom of God is defined by how we agree with and submit to Him, not in succeeding or accomplishing things in the world's eyes.

My success was in the agreement—God asking, "Are you willing to go to Nigeria?" "Yeah. I'm willing to go." "Are you willing to go to San Diego?" "Yeah. I'm willing to go." "Are you willing to have tough conversations with your wife, who you just married?" "Yeah. I'm willing to do that." Every time He has offered me an opportunity to grow, it started with me submitting and agreeing. Sometimes it takes humbling yourself, but it always leads to a better life.

Moving in faith and taking a leap of faith is great! But you had better not be taking that leap of faith with the belief that it will benefit you first. Then, you will be defined by the world's idea of success, and if you fall, you will feel that sting by the world's standards, too. Instead, we want to take that leap of faith to glorify Him, to benefit people, and to be able to give that knowledge away at some point to someone else who is on the journey of growth—whether they are your kids or someone else who looks up to you in life.

Jesus Came to Upgrade Our Decision-Making Process

The Bible clearly shows us that Jesus came to serve. Matthew 20:28 says that "the Son of Man did not come to be served, but to serve, and to give His life a ransom for many." This means that even when our world is flipped upside-down, or things may feel unstable, we have a model to learn from. He set the standard and reminds us that He continues to serve us with His love and strength, no matter what happens, in hopes we will do the same for others around us.

Isaiah 54:10 says,

> "For the mountains shall depart
> And the hills be removed,
> But My kindness shall not depart from you,
> Nor shall My covenant of peace be removed,"
> Says the LORD, who has mercy on you.

He says we are His family, and because of that, He treats us a certain way. When you're in covenant, meaning you're in agreement, there's a peace that can't be removed.

The passage goes on to say, "the Lord, who has compassion on you," meaning He has compassion on your mistakes. He has compassion for your anger. He has compassion for your grief. He has compassion for your confusion. The Holy Spirit wants to speak to us and counsel us, and He serves us with humility. He doesn't serve us because we make Him look good or we never let Him down; He serve us because He loves us.

That is a model to us. People are going to let us down. Situations are going to let us down. Our home environment is not always going to be the perfect, most conducive place for our growth. But those things we go through are not bigger than God. We can hope in His promises, and there is a love there that breaks off any spirit of fear and any yoke of shame.

That love can give us counsel if we lack wisdom. James 1:5 says that God gives wisdom generously. It says if any of us feel like we do not have wisdom for a situation, we should ask God. It does not say that we should ask the world, or ask our friend, or ask this person over here or there. Or seek it on social media, this news or that news—but the Good News (God's Word).

He gives generously to all without holding back because of our faults or lack or confusion. The fact of the matter is, we can put our belief in something else, and it may not turn out the way we want it to. But when we ask God, He serves us. He gives generously to all without finding fault; it's going to be given and there's no blame there. But it has to all start with being truthful, being honest with our struggles and our shortcomings. Most importantly, it has to begin with an honest yes in our hearts to Him.

He serves us by redeeming even the things we do wrong! First John 1:9 says, "If we confess our sins, He is faithful and just to forgive us *our* sins and to cleanse us from all unrighteousness." I love that. I love the fact that in His promises, we have the opportunity to establish a healthy foundation. We know that even when we make mistakes, grace and renewal are possible. There is an invitation to not stay stuck.

You can be healed first, and then that can be injected into your environment to change it, to help heal it in the name of the Lord. Quite frankly, we all know life can be very hard. Seeing and experiencing brokenness and emptiness can lead you to a bad place—to a breaking point. But God's plan is to put us in families who help keep us from those worst-case scenarios. He gives us all a choice about what to do—but not everyone uses that freedom to choose the good.

God is calling you up into your greatness. Jeremiah 29:11 says that God knows the plans He has for you. He does not have bad plans. He has plans to prosper you, not to harm you. He has plans to give you hope and a good future. It's really hard to accept that when the world is crumbling all around us, when we lose a family member to sickness or see racism. When we see injustice in life, it makes us angry. Some of it is righteous anger. But when you have these promises to cling to, it gives you hope. It gives you an opportunity to receive faith. It gives you access to healthy solutions. It offers you a chance to discuss things with people who disagree and open up opportunities to bring strength to a hurting society and the people you interact with daily. We get to show others that Jesus died so we can overcome. It gives you an opportunity to receive a breakthrough.

We as believers have promises that have been written. I believe the promises of Heaven have to be greater than the distractions of Hell in our lives. But sometimes we receive it the other way around. Sometimes we focus so much on the distractions of Hell that they seem greater than the promises of Heaven.

This is why Joshua 1:9 says, "Have I not commanded you? Be strong and of good courage; do not be afraid, nor be dismayed, for the LORD your God *is* with you wherever you go." And yet, if I'm being completely honest, it's hard to accept that truth at times because we *are* afraid. Sometimes we feel weak. Sometimes we don't feel worthy. Quite honestly, we don't feel strong or courageous.

Sometimes we feel like hiding in a private place so we can just cry out in fear. But the Word says "do not be afraid or be discouraged." Discouragement is another distraction of Hell. I know I was discouraged as a young boy because I didn't know my dad. Sometimes I would feel like I wasn't good enough to be loved. Or that I was not good enough to be a son, or that I wasn't successful enough. All these things I was telling myself were not only discouragements, they were lies.

Psalm 34:17 says, "*The righteous* cry out, and the LORD hears, and delivers them out of all their troubles." "The righteous" doesn't refer to just good people. "The righteous" refers to submitted people. "Righteous" means people who simply want to believe and cling to promises and hope.

We also read that if we delight in God, He will give us our hearts' desires. Some people feel like the desire will simply be their own success. They think it is saying they will get what they want for their ego. But the desire of your heart really is to be one with God, to be protected by Him, to be accepted and encouraged by Him, to be loved by Him. At the core, if you strip away all this stuff, the desire of your heart should be to be one with God. I want to be one with His peace and love.

Good Decisions Strengthen Families

God's design for family reminds us of His intentions for us. He has designed us to not be able to fully function as individuals on our own. We have to complement one another, submit to one another, serve one another. It's not for the dad to rule over the family, or for the mom to rule the family, or for the kids to run rampant. There has to be a healthy balance within a family. He designed us this way because He is this way; the Trinity mutually submits to and serves one another in harmony.

Sometimes we tend to give up on other family members or on

the hope that there can be peace in our homes. That there can be balance and alignment in the home. But God's design for a family sets us up with a healthy foundation and healthy decision-making in many different ways.

I'm not there to convert my family. That is the Holy Spirit's job. He's the One who does the converting. He's the One who offers an invitation for greater revelation of Jesus Christ and God the Father. But I get the privilege of reflecting Him.

In Colossians 3:18-21, Paul talks about wives submitting to their husbands, but he also says husbands should love their wives. He says children should obey their parents, and also that fathers should not provoke or dishearten their children. The interesting part is that the people in the family are all submitted to each other. It is not a one-way street where one person gets to do whatever they want.

You can't have a wife submitting to a husband if Christ is NOT IN that husband. Why? Because at that point, the husband tends to want to take the place of God in the relationship and rule over the woman instead of lifting her up, strengthening her, and coming alongside her. But when he is submitted to God, he tends to focus on how he can lift her up, and by doing so, she's able to submit to the God that lives inside her husband.

That becomes a reflection showing that the relationship is balanced. Only then can the couple really complement each other in their strengths and weaknesses. That reflects Heaven and the love of God to their children. The family gets an opportunity to steward their relationships with each other, and by doing so, it shows them how to love, how to serve, and how to come alongside each other.

Unfortunately, these days, it is very rare to find a family that is truly submitting to and complementing each other, especially in our society. We tend to focus on getting ahead more than getting alongside. We think that leading is you becoming something, you being the head of everything, as opposed to serving one another.

Quite frankly, when I was growing up, servant leadership was not modeled to me in my home. You might not have had that modeled to you either. Years ago, I came to a revelation that even when things aren't modeled correctly to you, you can still find them modeled correctly somewhere. When you see the right example, it will resonate with your spirit; you'll know it is good when you see it. There were lots of times when I went to different friends' homes and saw parents who really loved one another and served one another. Some of them were godly, some of them weren't, but from the outside looking in, it seemed they were growing together.

Even when they did argue, they knew how to take time to listen to one another and work it out as opposed to throwing their hands up and saying, "Hey, I give up." Healthy decision-making does not mean being in full agreement all the time, but it does mean wanting to come to a mutual understanding of what would be best for the home, best for the children, best for moving forward as a family unit. And probably most importantly, what is best long-term for those around you to learn from.

A home imparts great core values and principles to the children so that they will implement them in their own families later on. When we have a great understanding of what that looks like, we tend to grow. We become more patient in our home, we become more patient with our spouse (or single). We become more patient with our friends. We become more patient with ourselves in the maturation process of becoming a human being and as a follower of Jesus Christ. Our decision-making is impacted by that, because now we make decisions through a lens of the Kingdom of God. Jesus is our center. That is probably the greatest inheritance we can have or give.

When we make decisions through that lens, it doesn't mean they are always right, but at least there's a grace on it. So if we do mess up, we understand how to clean up our mess within the decision, or how to be patient with ourselves, knowing we are growing in that area. We can all get better at receiving and giving grace in the decision-making process.

Proverbs 22:6 says, "Train up a child in the way he should go, and when he is old he will not depart from it." This means they're going to go through life with certain traits, habits, and skill sets. They may get distracted here and there, but at the end of the day, the question in their hearts will always be: *What is the way I should go? Toward Jesus. Jesus is the way the truth and the life.* When you start to develop these core principles and core values, you can impart them to your children and start them off on the right foot in life.

What really got my attention as a kid were not necessarily things that were verbally spoken. It was the way people lived their lives. It was that there was a peace about their life that was very alluring and inviting. I found myself wanting to discover why they had that. Some modeled how to celebrate from a healthy space as opposed to a destructive space. They knew how to steward blessing, as well as how to deal with defeat. I learned how to walk through trials and tribulations from watching them.

I found more value when truth was being modeled to me as opposed to being told to me. I'd had a lot of great people say some really great things to me, but when the curtain was lifted up in their life, there was a lot of pain. There was a lot of loneliness. There was a lot of not being able to be open or vulnerable.

I felt like the ones who had peace had the ability to be vulnerable as well as truthful. That's what true freedom is to me. It is the fact that you can be vulnerable and truthful at the same time. You don't have to have your life together and look shiny from the outside. You can be vulnerable enough to say," Hey, I'm really struggling with this thing in my life. And I really have a hard time in this season in my life, but I know God's truth is gonna get me through. I know God's truth is going to get our family through. I know God's truth is going to help me through this situation that is really attacking me."

These are all things on which you can build a healthy foundation. I came to discover truth based on what was being modeled to me in other people's lives. I was able to have a full view of their life. It wasn't just a superficial thing. It was deep and very vulnerable. These people were just really at peace with who God was in their lives. I learned from them, got their perspective, and had the opportunity to ask them hard questions.

Making the Best Decisions

I've seen a lot of people make life-altering decisions. I've often seen them pressured into making decisions or trying to do things in their own power to get ahead. People often make decisions on the basis of trying to build themselves instead of others, or in an effort to be "social media famous" more than being socially and emotionally connected to their mission, function, and the calling on their lives.

Instant gratification is typically seen as more attractive than long-term principles of success and core values, things you can build your life upon. The problem is, if you're doing it for yourself and it's not working instantly, you will give up sooner. You will become more easily discouraged. You will feel like you are a failure if it doesn't work out right away. That is a heavy burden.

Sometimes we're anxious about certain things and we want to move quickly; we want instant success. That is not always as meaningful as we hope. That sometimes leaves us just as empty as before. I love what God's Word says in Philippians 4:6-7: that the "peace of God, which surpasses all understanding, will guard your hearts and minds through Christ Jesus." When we make decisions from peace and thanksgiving, we tend to have better outcomes.

If you're able to create a good filter for your decision-making process, you will have greater success. Again, success is not about achieving stuff. It is learning how to grow in the midst of the process, when things are good or bad.

True success is seeing the life and hope that comes from being submitted and serving. Do you complement other people's weaknesses, or do you call out that person's weaknesses? Do you strengthen that other person? Do you allow him or her to strengthen you? Are you vulnerable enough to be told you're wrong without getting offended?

Growing up, I believed I could draw the greatest attributes out of all the people I would meet in my lifetime and apply them to myself to become great. For example, I would think, "I admire this person's kindness." That person would become a role model of kindness to me. I would emulate that kindness and put it in my decision-making filter. It was a strategy that worked better than many other processes I could have used.

With God, I found my decision-making became a lot less complicated. When you don't understand who God is in your life, it's really hard to make a decision based on anything but your own opinion. But with God, you start to understand what it feels like to make decisions with Him. Because He is peace, you will feel peace. Because He is love, the decision will be made in love.

Initially, I had a lot of trial and error in this. It took a lot of research and development to understand what it felt like when I was making a decision from the Peace of God versus from my own striving. I came to find that when I was making decisions in my own strength, they were not the healthy ones. Maybe they were appealing to me, but they weren't best for the situation or for the people around me.

When you make decisions based on agreement with God and serving others, you become a benefactor of God's grace and mercy. There's a favor and a grace that rests on your decision. Even when you mess up, there's grace. For example, even when I got pushback from my family about moving to San Diego, I knew in my heart that the decision was not about me, it was about God and my family.

I don't get it right all the time. Sometimes I can become a little self-righteous and think because I am doing things for God, that makes me right. That is not how it works! But if we stay faithful to His presence, faithful to the calling on our lives, and honor Him in our decision-making, then our future tends to have more hope. When the choice is unclear, we have the opportunity to ask Him for more clarity.

Isaiah 40:29 says, "He gives power to the weak, and to *those who have* no might He increases strength." There will be seasons in all our lives when we might not be fortunate enough to be in a good situation. We will feel weak. Maybe we're trying to grow up without a father or having problems related to work or finances. Maybe there is just a situation that is not healthy in general. No matter what, God's promises allow us to strengthen ourselves in Him. His faithfulness and unfailing love will be a constant guide for us, even in our bumbling around.

That is true even when we are facing trials and tribulations. We read in Isaiah 40:31 that when we put our hope in God, our strength is renewed. That we will feel like we are soaring on wings like eagles do! It says as we hope in Him, we will feel like we can run without getting tired. Our strength will not be depleted when we put our hope in God.

When you make life-altering decisions, your decision-making process should have these markers in them to help you see how you are growing as a human being. At the end of the day, the whole purpose of your existence is to glorify God. God is just as powerful in your failures as He is in your successes—even more so, because people can identify even more closely with you and Christ in your failures. They can identify with being sad. They can identify with loss and disappointment. They can identify with falling on their face and having to learn from that.

You don't want to lean just on your own thinking and understanding. You want to submit all your ways to God. Proverbs 3:5-6 says,

> Trust in the LORD with all your heart,
> And lean not on your own understanding;
> In all your ways acknowledge Him,
> And He shall direct your paths.

The blessing is always wrapped in the submission and the obedience unto God. Direction comes from that posture.

God would like us to understand that He's the one we have to lean on constantly. I can tell you this right now: I have not arrived by any means. I don't think we arrive until God calls us home, but I do believe that as you're on this journey in life, as long as you're real with the Lord and with the people around you, you will start to see a real progression, growth, and freedom in your own life.

CHAPTER
ten

{ Our Inheritance }

Most of us have never received a big inheritance. Maybe we dream about one. Wouldn't it be nice to find out we are related to someone who left us money that could change our lives? Most of us know that is not likely. A big inheritance is seldom a possibility for us in the natural world—but the Bible clearly says that when we become a part of God's family, a pretty epic inheritance comes along with it! First John 3:1 says, "Behold what manner of love the Father has bestowed on us, that we should be called children of God! Therefore the world does not know us, because it did not know Him." Romans tells us if we are children of God, we are joint heirs with Christ.

I think we can start to get a new idea of what inheritance looks like through the Bible. That has been my source for reestablishing and rewiring my mind and my heart. Inheritance is so much more than money; it is counsel and wisdom when we need it. Inheritance means we do not have to be slaves to the ways of this world; we can be free and full of faith. Our inheritance is Jesus and connection to God, who has made all things! Essentially, it is receiving something that you don't necessarily deserve because someone else has already paid the price for it and has entrusted it to you because of your relationship.

Inheritance Comes Through Relationship

In Colossians 3:23, Paul says that whatever we do, we are to work hard, as if we are doing it for God, not for men. When we do this, we receive an inheritance as our reward. The greatest revelation of inheritance for me was that as long as I felt like I was working unto the Lord, I was going to have the opportunity to receive great things because of my relationship with Him. Often that great thing was His peace, even if I didn't particularly like the work. My reward is often His presence, His peace, and purpose. I can receive meaning and hope, and that's honestly the greatest form of inheritance that we can ever get. The goodness that comes from His presence and peace is what most people hope money, power, or status will give them—but they usually don't in the end.

When you start to do things just to please other people, it seems like you are almost on a hamster wheel. You constantly run and run and run with no fulfillment. There's no reward. You can never get enough of what you are looking for. You are always going to feel like you need to do more in order to receive approval. This usually leads to burnout. It can also open the door for your heart to be trampled upon when you are not affirmed in your efforts.

But if you do things unto the Lord and not unto man, you have a greater opportunity to receive your inheritance from the Lord. Sometimes on the outside it looks the same. However, internally in your heart you are actually being fulfilled on the right premises. You are being fulfilled with what He has in store for your life, not what society has. You can work your normal job and know in your heart that you are working for the Lord, and your work will have more peace, joy, and fulfillment that releases your true inheritance from God!

What is Your True Inheritance?

Your inheritance is a greater understanding of Him and His eternal grace and love in your life. It is a greater understanding of peace and patience with yourself and others. It is really good to do things at God's pace because His is the most observant pace. You observe more about yourself, your faith, who you are, what you really believe, who He is to you—all that stuff gets reestablished in your heart. You walk away with greater understanding of and love for who He is. More importantly, you walk away with greater tools to help equip others on their journey through life.

The inheritance you receive is essentially a deeper covenant relationship and understanding of the Lord in your life. I believe that's what inheritance is: a greater revelation of the promises God has for us, and a deeper understanding of how He wants to be close to us. The promises that God has already spoken over us are obtainable even when our lives are a complete mess.

The best thing about the inheritance God has for us is that there's nothing we personally can do to qualify for it. He's not a father who makes us earn it or who judges us for not being worthy. Colossians 1:12 says to thank God that He qualified you to share in the inheritance. He's already qualified us!

It's not about being His favorite. In a natural family, sometimes the favorite gets more. In God's family, we are all favorites. There is more than enough for us all. Sharing in the inheritance is simply aligning ourselves with a Father who deeply loves us. It is knowing that His spirit—the same spirit that raised Christ from the dead—lives inside us. All of the revelation of God, along with these promises, is the inheritance—and a GREAT one at that! These promises are the things that allow us to get through our hard days and to really push through when we're questioning ourselves, questioning our purpose, or even when we're questioning God. It will allow us to go deeper and see His faithfulness and goodness in our lives.

There is some drama involved here, too. Just as normal inheritances usually have some drama going on if they are big or life-changing, the enemy is going to be there trying to rob us of this revelation. Different distractions will come disguised as fulfillment or temporary substitutes for peace.

In Luke 4, Jesus fasts for forty days. He goes into the wilderness, where He's tempted by the devil himself! The devil tries to offer Jesus things that are less than what God has, but which are more immediate. He tries to steal Jesus's identity; then he tries to steal His worship; then he tries to rob Him of His knowledge of the truth. In all three instances, Jesus keeps hitting him with the promises that God has spoken over His life and through His Word.

The Bible says that the devil took him up and showed him all the kingdoms of the world at the time. And he said, "If you will bow down and worship me, I'll give this all to you." It's funny because in Luke 1:33 it talks about Jesus and that there will be "no end of His kingdom." So what the enemy tried to do was get him to exchange an inheritance with no end for something that was temporary! How many of us have been tempted and forced to make a choice? I know I have, and before God came into my life, my choices were not good.

The same thing happened in the Garden of Eden. It is the story of mankind. And there was a choice that had to be made there, but Adam and Eve chose the inheritance of the enemy—which was a fallen world, sin, and death. It was life apart from God and the beautiful abundance in the Garden. They were tempted by the enemy to give it away for momentary fulfillment and a false promise. And just like that, the enemy took away mankind's inheritance. But Jesus came and died for us to give it back to us if we want it.

Unfortunately, in our own homes, for whatever reason, we see this as well. Many of our fathers have abandoned their responsibilities to raise their own kids. They have traded the inheritance they could give their kids for temporary pleasure, leaving behind the great opportunity to train up the young child's heart and mind that they have been entrusted with. They have basically given away their inheritance, just like Esau did in the Bible. Esau gave away his entire inheritance, birthright, and identity for a bowl of soup. He couldn't see past the moment. He was hungry in the moment, and to meet that hunger, he was willing to give away his entire future! Many of us have fallen victim to this same deception. I know I did at one point.

The devil always wants us to trade our rich inheritance for something that's temporary. He wants us to relinquish something eternal for something that is momentary. But Jesus showed us that we all have an opportunity to make a choice, to stick with our birthright (relationship with God) even when there is temptation to give it up for momentary pleasures or easier decisions. He knows it is hard; however, He showed us we can do it and He can help us! We might be tempted to give up long-term inheritance and generational growth for short-term pleasures and short-term thinking. However, that leaves our society, culture, and families bankrupt. Then we find ourselves trying to fill voids with things that can be very unhealthy for us.

The Invitation to Inheritance

The inheritance is an invitation. It is not automatic. We have to choose to align with it. However, when we do, we get the gift of receiving a peace that surpasses all understanding and meekness that brings strength and life. Psalm 37:11 says "the meek shall inherit the earth, and shall delight themselves in the abundance of peace." Now that is an inheritance!

All these promises that we get a chance to keep are all for us to reflect God's glory. Yet in this world it is the opposite: an earthly inheritance usually is for the benefit of the recipient. It is not usually for the good of others, and it always comes at a high cost. We usually have to wait for someone to die before that inheritance is released to us.

Inheritance means you receive a blessing you did not work for or earn. It was given to you by grace. If you manage it well and have a strong understanding of what you received, you might think of how you can use it to honor the person who left it to you.

I think the inheritance that we get in Jesus, when walking in His goodness, offers us an invitation to honor Him and what He has given us. We can do that through our actions and words with everybody that we encounter. We can also do that by being humble enough to grow in areas where we lack maturity. The beauty of this inheritance is that no matter where you were born, what situation you were born into, or the terrible way people might have treated you, there still is hope. You still have a full right to this inheritance because of what Christ did.

That inheritance comes through grace. We all would have inherited the Garden of Eden (being one with God) if it were not for sin. We do not deserve a good inheritance anymore because of sin. But Jesus comes and says we do deserve it because He restores our relationship to our Father through His death and resurrection in our lives.

If anything, this inheritance offers you a greater invitation to come closer to the source of life Himself. Our Father in Heaven has spoken promises over our lives, promises over our destiny and the journey that He has for us. It may not feel like that at times, but it's in those hard moments that we really see our inheritance come alive. However, that perception is developed along the journey when we say yes to the process.

These provinces are for people who are desiring closeness with Him. That is God's heart in the middle of all this: that anytime we are able to lay our own thinking down, or lay our life down to follow God, that's when we start to see what greater love is all about. In John 15:13 the Bible says there is no greater love than someone laying down his own life for the life of one of his friends. That's God's heart!

His heart is that we understand how to lay down our lives for others. Song of Songs 2:4 says that His banner over us is love. That's God's heart for us. However, if you have never been introduced to this love, it's only natural to have a hard time receiving it in your mind or heart, especially if you come from a home where you were abandoned, abused, or if you have had a very rough life.

The Holy Spirit is Our Inheritance

As we accept the inheritance Jesus died to give us, we inherit a Counselor—Someone to walk alongside us on this journey toward the way, the truth, and the life. This is the Holy Spirit of God. We are able to be one with the Spirit and ask for His comfort, help, and counsel when we have to make decisions and don't know the way to go. That is something money cannot buy!

We can also ask Him to help us identify limiting beliefs and remind us of the truth about why those do not apply to us. So when there is a belief like, "I'm another statistic" or "It will never get better" or "I won't get the same opportunity as someone else," the Holy Spirit can help us notice this thinking, then align our hearts and mind with the promises of God over our lives. If we are falling into the victim mentality, He can remind us that in God we have a victorious mentality! This is our inheritance in the way, the truth, and the life.

Even in hardship, we can have a mentality of victory because Christ is in the center. This really reshaped my whole thinking. I never have to feel alone in a situation . However, if I do, I actually can tap into God's heart for me and *know* I'm not alone. It reestablishes faith, reestablishes confidence, and reestablishes hope in my heart— hope that God wants to do some phenomenal things in my life moving forward. He desires that for all His children, including you reading this book!

The Holy Spirit is with us. He's fulfilling us and He's redeeming areas within us that might need repair, if we want Him to. When we make a decision or ask for counsel, He gives us an answer that comes not from shame or judgment but out of redemption, grace, and love. That's a humbling, crazy, and beautiful thing all wrapped up in the journey.

For example, I was leading a counseling session one time with someone in the military. This man had had a terrible childhood. Growing up for him was like growing up in a living hell. The fact that he was even alive was a miracle. All that trauma, all that abuse, and all the things that he saw were overwhelming, as they would be for anyone. It broke him. He didn't know what love looked like from a father, even though he had an earthly father in his life. He was so desperate and broken that he resorted to some very dark things to try to fill the void and get some happiness and peace in his life. He was so sad and depressed; he would say it was as if all the color had been washed out of his life. He once said that even though the sun had risen, he didn't see any light. His soul had really taken a thrashing.

These wounds prompted him to make some really horrible decisions in his life and cause a tremendous amount of pain to others around him.

He didn't know how to treat a woman well or show her that he wanted to be with her long-term. He didn't know how to love a woman because no one had ever showed him. He was trying, and he was failing in his own standard. It caused him to lose a lot of friendships, to lose a lot of himself. He essentially became callous to receiving or understanding love. Because of that, he was caught in a lot of oppression and a lot of depression—because love is the only thing that can set you free from that. It caused him to go into an even deeper spiral of making mistakes and poor decisions. He was in a VERY dark space in his life.

As we took inventory of his life, he caught a huge breakthrough! He realized that in order for him to experience freedom, he had to embrace forgiveness. He also had to embrace forgiveness for others as well. He received God on the spot and immediately, healing came rushing in as an inheritance to his obedience and step of faith. When we receive God, we get access to wisdom and restoration that we didn't even know was available! Wisdom that causes us to break cycles and lead us to a better inheritance and legacy for our earthly family. Broken families no longer have to be broken and fatherless. People who have not had fathers can become sons and heirs. They can receive a new understanding. The mistakes and wrongs of the past no longer have to define the future. We can receive inheritance and different promises if we are able to submit ourselves to the Lord unconditionally.

We receive revelation of God's heart and what God's heart says about us, that He's a gracious and compassionate Father, that He's slow to anger and He's abounding in love—even to all of us who have fallen way short in our lives. This is one of the greatest starting points toward the way, the truth, and the life.

Faith and Freedom Are Our Inheritance

We also inherit faith. I used to think I had to do things to create a feeling of faith. But actually, our inheritance is that we do not have to strive or do a bunch of stuff to be accepted or to feel loved. Knowing this changed my view of faith.

I realized the more I engage with others around me with a heart to bless them and not get anything in return, I am able to model a deposit mindset rather than a withdrawal mindset. I am starting from a place of having more than enough already! I used to feel I never had enough, but in faith, I see I have more than I need, and I can give it away to others who feel empty.

A deposit mindset says, "I'm here to give you something and not seek anything in return." A withdrawal mindset says, "I want to be close to you or have a relationship with you because I'm trying to get something from you." I used to have a withdrawal mindset, thinking only about how other people could help me get ahead. I would meet someone, and my first thought would be, "What can they do for me? How can they bless me? How can they make me feel happy?"

A deposit mindset says, "How can I ensure you are better, stronger, and happier from knowing or interacting with me?" Sometimes that may be a word of encouragement, whether it's just sitting there talking, laughing, joking, or just listening to their heart. Maybe sometimes it's sitting and listening when we disagree with that person or position. That is a lost art in our society today.

If we know our inheritance, we know we come from a place of more than enough, and that leads us to freedom because we don't need anything from the other person. This is what my friend showed me as he cheered for the team even when we were losing. He didn't need the team to cheer him up—he was there to cheer them up! He was there with a deposit mindset, not a withdrawal mindset. This mindset and freedom are discovered in the Lord Himself.

This freedom is one way we can show faith to people around us. By receiving Jesus Christ as our Lord and Savior and being filled with the Holy Spirit, we get the opportunity to live from abundance every single day—even on the toughest day of our life. And that should give us hope! There's always an opportunity! The Bible says in Galatians 4:7 that we were living like slaves before Christ came. We were slaves to the things of this world, to the thinking of this world, to the narrative of this world—slaves to act certain ways based on the bad things that were done to us. The verse goes on to say that we are now heirs with Christ and we can live free from the ways of the world. He sets us free from serving the world and allows us the freedom to pursue Him and be free of slavery to a world that is not kind, a world that has taken from us and hurt us.

We're no longer slaves, but sons. And if we are sons, then we are heirs through God. Once I figured out that I'm not just a son of the best Father, but an heir to everything He has made and done, it really opened up my thinking and replaced my limiting beliefs.

Like writing this book, for example. There's no way in a billion years that I thought I would be able to write a book, especially on something that has impacted my life so deeply: not having a father in my home. I also never thought I would write a book about God and how He transformed my life. The fact that you are even reading this is a miracle to me! I did not grow up in the church, y'all!! So if the way, the truth, and the life has been given to me to take away my shame, pain, and all the other crap, I know undoubtedly you can receive the same inheritance.

I am free now. Free of the shame and pain that came from that because of my new inheritance. Receiving your inheritance can do the same for you. Honestly, the sky's the limit for what you can do if you choose to go on the journey.

Freedom also lets you not react to everything others do. Over the last few years, I have found that even though I am a believer and follower of Jesus Christ, there were still areas of my heart that needed to be healed in a deeper way. Oh yeah, I am still a work in progress—we all are. There are areas of my heart where I say, "Oh, that hurts," or "That rubbed me the wrong way." But those are invitations to say, "God, why is this making me feel this way? What is Your plan for freedom here in my heart?" It's a really beautiful thing to be unoffended when you should take offense. When you can choose not to take it because it doesn't serve you, that is freeing. That is liberating. That is yours to inherit as well.

Redemption Is Our Inheritance

Redemption is another inheritance God has given us. When I make boneheaded decisions or say something that's not of God, I can fix it. In the past, I was afraid to admit wrong because I was very influenced by what others thought of me, so I found myself trying to control their perceptions of me.

With our inheritance we are able to be humble enough and genuine enough to apologize and grow from our mishaps. God can redeem every mistake or misstep and help lead us into greater maturity. We get the privilege of receiving even more of His inheritance! We also get the opportunity to manage what we already have been entrusted with, which leads to potential increase.

A part of our inheritance is tied to the marvelous privilege of showing others that God redeems. To show people that they also have an inheritance that can change their life! God redeemed my past to show others that no matter what they are up against, or what their past was like, He can turn it around and give them something greater. I wasn't given an earthly "right" to do what I am doing. I didn't go to seminary. I didn't go to an institution to study theology. But in God's grace He still is using me to teach others about Him. I have encouraging news regarding that: He feels the same about you!

God can go far above and beyond our expectations for our lives. Ephesians 1:7 says that we have redemption through His blood, the forgiveness of our trespasses, according to the riches of His grace. It's not something that we have to work for; it has come by faith through grace.

No one is so far out that they cannot experience the redemption of God. No matter where you're at in the world, there is redeeming hope for your life, if you simply say yes. Colossians 1:14 says "we have redemption through His blood, the forgiveness of sins." Even when we don't believe that He is still sending redemption! Psalm 111:9 says that "He has sent redemption to his people."

We can have Heaven here on Earth by simply saying yes to Him. And the capacity for His redeeming power is far greater than what we thought or can ever imagine.

I know some of you reading this may be thinking about your own lives and saying, "Man, what did I do to deserve this?" Maybe you've been beaten down and broken by life and people in it.

By just receiving Christ and filling yourself up with His presence, you're justified by His grace as a gift to you through redemption. There is nothing you can do to earn it; no matter how hard you work; you can never earn more inheritance. God's capacity for redemption is strictly a gift to us.

Our trespasses, the things that we've done, things that we may have allowed our hearts to receive, or we have inherited unintentionally—there's forgiveness for all that. Luke 21:28 says, "Now when these things begin to happen, look up and lift up your heads, because your redemption draws near." We should straighten up and raise our heads even in our darkest moments. Sometimes our heads are pointed down, looking at things of this world, looking over here, looking to the left, looking to the right, looking at our circumstances. God said we should lift our heads, meaning we should lift our countenances up toward Him so that He can pour His countenance over us because our redemption is drawing near.

What does that mean? Our redemption not only draws near when we get called home to be in His presence, but our redemption draws near now. Even in this time, we can be redeemed—even if we have deep wounds and pain and loss, we can be redeemed. This has developed in my life over the last few years as a result of this revelation. The deeper we go, and the more willing we are to really humble ourselves and submit, the more we start to see that God really wants to take us to another level. It is not just for our freedom and for our benefit; we have the opportunity to impact and benefit others. Again, having a deposit mindset over a withdrawal mindset.

Our Inheritance Allows Hope, Gratitude, and Growth

An inheritance in the natural world could bring hope and gratitude and be used for growth. It is the same with the inheritance that we receive through Christ. So how does this happen? Mostly through our engagement with the Word of God.

That doesn't mean that just reading the Bible changes everything. You have to read it, digest it, and then apply it to your life. You have to apply it to your journey of what it means to follow God. First Chronicles 16:34 says, "Oh, give thanks to the LORD, for *He is* good! For His mercy *endures* forever." Even if our love does not endure for Him, even if we have a terrible day, even if we walk away or we get upset, His love and hope endure. When you are a Hot Mess Express, there is still love for you. It shows you the abounding love that God has. This love makes a way for growth and positive change that is not possible without love from someone outside of you, cheering you on and telling you there is still a good future for you.

Maybe we have lost family members, or maybe we have been deeply hurt, abused, or abandoned. The tragedy of all these things can snatch the gratitude from the soil of our lives and cause us to fall into self-protection if we do not know God as our protector. So we protect ourselves by building a wall, and that wall keeps us from being really grateful and happy. Gratitude is one of the best feelings in the world. It is also a position of combat, spiritually, when dark things come against us.

I experienced a lot of negative things in my life, and it caused me to have callousness in my heart. I didn't have hope or gratitude. It eroded away any small portion I may have had. It also caused me to have callousness in my growth, and new opportunities stopped flowing in my life. I was stuck in life and couldn't understand why. It was one of the most helpless feelings I ever faced. It really prevented me from growing. However, after fully surrendering, redemption started to occur. It started with humble surrender and admitting that I needed help. According to Romans 5:8 God demonstrates His love for us because when we were all sinners, He still died for us!

When we receive our inheritance, we can not only get unstuck, we can help others do the same. The growth does not stop with us. We continue to lay down our lives for the people in our world and community. It's not just laying our lives down for another person, but laying down our lives and submitting them to God to find out the deeper things about Him that releases our inheritance. And that causes you to bless your friends, too.

You become better at strengthening your friends and situations, and you can edify any circumstances you are thrust into. You can bring the Kingdom of Heaven into the midst of that. When we allow ourselves to be in that role, we help other people so they won't have to endure the same hardship we did and become callous in their own hearts.

Spiritual Inheritance, Favor and Maturity

As we grow, we not only become recipients of God's inheritance for us, but we also leave an inheritance for others to pick up. Again, not just an inheritance for one day when we die, but an inheritance that we can pass on to others as they see us walking in our maturity as human beings. They can see what we carry, and they can start to carry it as well. That inheritance is a free gift that is simply received by accepting and embracing Christ in your process of growth for your life. This is partly how we make deposits in the lives of others: by modeling what it is like to walk in that free inheritance.

The spiritual inheritance that I desire to leave to others is the fact that they do not have to abandon the process of growing close to the Lord even when things get tough (because they will, I promise).

My prayer is to leave a spiritual inheritance for my family that impacts my children, their children, their children's children, etc. That's what I hope to impart to my children as they grow older: that their hopes, their fears, their doubts, their triumphs, and their celebrations should all be rooted in God. The fact that I can come from not having an inheritance from an earthly father, and through God, to offer my own children an inheritance of love and presence is evidence of the goodness, redemption, and mercy of God.

When you are walking in that inheritance, you start to grow into maturity. What does that look like? It looks like loving the Lord with all your heart, soul, and mind. It looks like 1 Peter 4:8, which says, "above all things have fervent love for one another." Love covers a multitude of sins. We all will make mistakes. We will fall on our face, we will say things we didn't want to say, we will do things we didn't mean to do, but we can always come back to being grounded in love, and that love can redeem us from our bad decisions. Does it mean there won't be repercussions for your decisions? No. Yet there is hope in the aftermath of those bad decisions. I pray that I get a chance to impart that knowledge to my children and the people around me all my living days, so that others would give the goodness of God's presence an opportunity to add strength and clarity to their lives.

I think David in the Bible modeled this well. Obviously, he was a great king, and he was anointed, but he also understood honor. He understood repenting (confessing and being honest), and he understood God's grace and mercy. So when he messed up, he came back around. It wasn't just something he read about. He modeled that to the people around him.

I can't imagine being told that you were going to be the king of all of Israel as a teenager, and that your first assignment would be to serve the person who is going to torment you over the next several years of your life, trying to kill you and forcing you to run and hide. But even when David had the opportunity to kill the person who was trying to kill him, he didn't do it because he trusted and was submitted to God, His ways, and His timing.

It took time for David to come into his assignment. There was a maturity that grew. In David's case, he matured in the favor of God by receiving the anointing from Samuel. Then he also grew in the favor of man by the way he carried himself among the people.

God said David was a man after His own heart. He said this even in his failures!! This spiritual inheritance was birthed out of a journey submitted to the Lord. This should give us all hope. It means that when we make mistakes, there is still hope for redemption.

With time and consistency, you can start to see the results in your life. What in your life produces the best results in the people around you? The fruit of your life should point to the roots in your life. One of the most powerful things we can do is get to know God and submit our hearts to Him. In doing so, we start to be conformed to His image from the inside out. When we consistently seek His heart, we find new layers of inheritance and new strength to accept it, and a life of power, freedom, and love.

CHAPTER
eleven

{ Our Destiny }

estiny can be defined by many things, but one is what brings us joy throughout our lifetime. What brings our hearts to life? Our destiny could be to raise a phenomenal family and have children, or to be the CEO of a Fortune 500 company. Whatever your destiny, it will be unique to you, and you will be uniquely equipped for it. You also will have a unique journey into that destiny.

Destiny seems to feel fullest when it's aligned with what we believe God has in store for our lives, as well as helping others thrive and grow. We get the honor to walk with others through tough seasons in their lives.

I also discovered destiny, strangely, in mistakes I have made, failures I've had, curiosities that have stirred my mind, the times I was forced to make a decision and actually made the wrong one. Destiny was defined even in those moments. Strangely enough, I learned to appreciate the journey even more through these tough seasons.

Destiny is honed over the course of time. There are a lot of things we'll get a chance to do in our lives, but not all of those opportunities will necessarily be right for us.

Also, there will be some opportunities that you don't want to take but know you should—and those could be the ones that bring you a sense of peace and purpose. If you had told me I was going to be a pastor for a season of my life, never in a million years would I have thought I would be qualified or even have the knowhow or passion to do it. But that wasn't a disqualifier in God's eyes; if anything, it was *the* qualifier.

I feel I came into my destiny when I just submitted to God's purpose. I had a great encounter in which He forgave me, an encounter that built me up and edified me, an encounter that embraced me, even when I no longer embraced myself—even when I embraced the wrong labels for my life.

My encounter with God gave me a sense of peace. I thought, "OK, I have a starting point." It did not allow me to think, "I'm good now." But it gave me something greater. It gave me a starting point I could actually start building upon. And it took the pressure off; I didn't have to be perfect or arrive at a certain standard before coming to God.

There are still days when I make mistakes. However, there is grace and redirection when I choose to seek them. I'm thankful that grace redeems me—and where grace is, faith starts to arise. That faith and that grace allow me to come into a place of freedom. They will allow you to do the same. My life's purpose is to point other people toward the fact that there is hope for their lives as well if they choose—and for the ones who've already accepted Jesus and have a relationship with God, to encourage them to press in for what God has for their lives.

My destiny involves doing that for people who don't believe in God, people who are far off, people who have a background like mine, people who were fatherless like me, people who may be a minority like myself. I just love the fact that when we come into destiny, God's promises start really speaking over our hearts and into our lives, and start guiding our paths and leading our steps.

Before I met God, my work was focused on making money. My work was unto survival. My work was unto trying to make sure others did not judge me. But for real? I don't want to live that life. Would you? We actually have access to a more fulfilling purpose.

Keys to Your Destiny: Having a Servant Heart
Proverbs 16:3 says that if you commit whatever you do to God, your plans will be established and you will succeed. As I committed my work to the Lord, my plans were established—but it didn't happen overnight. It was a journey and as I went on it, the plan started to get established more and more. I started to see success redefined in a healthy way. Job 23:14 says, "For He performs *what is* appointed for

me, and many such *things are* with Him." So I learned that He already has things planned for me. He already has destiny appointed to me, and I just need to come into alignment with it. I am so encouraged by this, and I hope you are as well.

Does this mean I have to do a lot of things and try to clamor for my destiny? No, it's actually the opposite. I get a chance to reflect that love that has already been appointed to me. It's a free gift that was entrusted to me to share with the rest of the world, including you reading this.

My passion was definitely stoked by serving others. When I was living in a really small town in Washington, my life and purpose were not dedicated to the Lord. I only thought about what I was going to be doing professionally, how I was going to get ahead, how I was going to fulfill my dreams. Don't get me wrong, having goals and dreams is not a bad thing. However, they consumed my attitude, thinking, and daily living in an unhealthy way.

I thought everybody in that town was against me. I had no friends, I had no allies. I had all enemies (in my mind), and that isolated me. It did not prompt my heart to serve others, which led to probably one of the most depressing seasons of my life. It also caused me to not embrace community or relationships with others. I had no desire to grow by coaching or volunteering with kids; I was too focused on myself and my professional basketball career to see others.

Oddly, deep down I had a desire to help kids and coach when I was done playing, but I truly was too prideful to express that desire to others around me. In all honesty, I probably had more basketball experience than all the other coaches in that small town combined, but in my pride I felt they should be reaching out to me instead of me reaching out to them. This lack of humility isolated me even more. I had experience and a gift for the game of hoops, but my attitude and perspective were so selfish. I don't think I would have added any strength or value to the community at that time because my attitude was not appropriate for it. I didn't have the foresight or wisdom to see how to use my experiences and gifts to serve the community.

Do you believe you have a gift and can offer something greater to the people around you? I believe you do, and so does God. However, we need to have the appropriate attitude and heart posture before stepping into a new blessing for our lives.

When I gave my life to God, I knew it was no longer about me. It was going to be about glorifying God, growing as a person, and helping others around me. However, I didn't know where to start, and honestly, I was still being redeemed from the shame I was carrying around from my past. I was on a journey of redemption in my personal life and deeply desired to help others, but I really didn't know what that looked like. But I was walking by faith and seeking truth.

It started with repentance (admitting my mess), followed by acceptance (accepting the Lord as savior in my life), followed by redemption (the journey of repair in areas of my life that needed care). These steps allowed me to come into a place where I understood that life was no longer about me. It also gave me a pathway to walk along that I could share with others. It was about God and it was about other people.

My attitude of pride was one of the first things that changed in my life. It was very liberating to discover that I was the cause of my own growth restrictions. I finally understood why I had been feeling so empty and unfulfilled. When I started to walk in faith, by simply being obedient to the Lord I inherited some breakthrough in my life. Here is the best part about that: it's available for you as well!

Let me give you an example: while living in Washington, someone approached me about coaching a local eighth-grade girls basketball team. I was asked to apply, and told I would have a "high probability" of getting the job with no problem (basically guaranteeing me the job). I was a bit cocky about it, thinking, "Oh, I got this job, and honestly I'm WAY overqualified to do this, but I'll do it." In my mind, there was no way they could tell me no. My heart wasn't right at all. I was probably the most qualified person in that region to do that job, but I almost felt like it was a little bit beneath me—which was super arrogant and prideful.

Let me tell you, that attitude will ruin more opportunities for you than anything. That was a wrong heart posture to have, I was not thinking of how I could serve those young girls and their families. I was not thinking about the young kids and their needs. I was thinking about my ego, my qualifications, my pride. Me, me, me!!

I ended up not getting the job, and that really threw me for a loop. I was incredibly upset, embarrassed, confused, and disappointed.

A couple of months went by, and then someone approached me about applying for the head coaching position for the varsity boys basketball team in town. This was one of the top jobs for the school, and definitely a bigger responsibility to handle. I'm not going to lie; I was hesitant because I didn't want to be told no again. I discovered in that moment that I had a fear (stronghold) of rejection. I didn't want to deal with the shame or the idea that I wasn't good enough. Little did I know that was something I personally had struggled with since childhood. It was preventing my growth as a human being. It reminded me of the rejection I felt from not knowing my dad, times when my mom would say rejecting things to me, times when I looked to others for acceptance and got the opposite.

I carried that "spirit of rejection" into my adulthood. When I was asked to apply for the vasity job, I had a revelation that I was wounded and didn't even know it.

I applied hesitantly for the job, but with a new humility after falling flat on my face the first time. I ended up GETTING the job, and my passion to help kids not only grew in the sport of basketball, but probably more importantly in the game of life. I had a sense of being born to do that. I got to coach basketball and share my faith, not by what I was saying but more importantly, how I was living. You have to understand: this was a VERY small, predominantly white town. I was one of only three minority males there). Also, none of the kids on the team were believers in God or had been introduced to faith. I was a new believer, and the school was a public school, not a Christian school. So I had to get creative about how I would share my faith with these kids and the other coaches in a secular school system. I did it by simply speaking the language of service and love to the kids, their families, and my peers.

Initially, the kids' hearts were hard, and their mentality was one of constant defeat. They were used to being defeated both on and off the court. They were used to dealing with stuff in their lives and having to live in a small town where most people knew their struggles. Sports was their only outlet, the only safe haven they had to really enjoy life. But the team had lost every game for the last three years straight. It was uniquely challenging to help redeem their morale, both athletically and personally.

I was trusted to become their leader. I already had my experience in hoops as a platform to speak into their athletic ability. Yet with my newfound faith in God, I also had a platform to speak into their hearts as young people. So I used those platforms to build their personal wellness first. I wasn't necessarily concerned about wins and losses at the outset. I was more concerned with their mental, physical, and internal wellness. I was concerned with the transformation of their hearts and how they would grow to become great parents, great businesspeople and entrepreneurs. I wanted them to have fun while they were competing, to enjoy the process of working hard as they were becoming better people and athletes. I wanted them to have fun learning and being around their teammates and families.

I didn't even realize at the time that I was teaching them about the Kingdom of God.

That attitude changed those kids tremendously—and that stoked a fire and a passion in me to better understand how serve others. It also change my perception of my environment. I didn't know that God was priming and preparing me for what I would be doing down the line on a grander scale with people of influence—people in the sports industry, the political world, leaders of business networks and churches. He was teaching me to serve, not from a place of offense from not knowing my own dad or of feeling like I was abandoned, but by the grace of God. He was teaching me that I could serve from a place of security, hope, and love.

Then my sense of purpose started to grow. It helped me to prioritize my dreams and goals. I realized my self-focused dreams would never fulfill me, but the ones to help others would actually change the world. The dreams that caused me to be really committed to helping people and glorifying God—those were the ones that made me come alive.

Those dreams also gave me great opportunities to meet some phenomenal people. In doing that, my dreams and goals started to change. I started to see things through the lens of how Christ served me, how Christ died for me, and how I can die to my selfishness, serve others, love God, then actually make an impact. Even if the people we are serving aren't influential on a global scale, regardless of whether we live in a remote town or a big city, we have the ability to make a difference. We can make a difference if we have very few resources or a lot at our fingertips. Wherever we are, our ability to make a difference starts with a heart posture, followed by a mindset, driven by an agenda that is pure.

We have to be honest when trying to serve others in the name of God. Although our intentions may be good, our actions, approach, and speech can affect our impact and perceived authenticity. If we start to feel frustrated and impatient when we don't see the desired results, or we start to think the person we are serving is not of value to God, or wonder why we should even pray for them, those are big red flags that our motives are no longer pure and have become about us. That can lead to us inadvertently villainizing the people we're serving in our hearts. That's a trap for people of faith.

Having a sense of purpose gave me a better understanding of how to serve others, no matter where they were in life or if they had faith or not. It also helped me identify some new healthy goals for my own life. One of them is writing this book and sharing the heart of what it means to be repaired and redeemed from a fatherless home or an "against all odds" situation. If that sounds like you or someone you know, just understand that nothing is impossible. God can walk with you as your Father. He can also walk with you as a Friend, Counselor, Provider, and Protector. I have seen this occur in my own life, and am thankful that it's also available to you.

Keys to Your Destiny: Staying Connected When Times Are Hard
One of the biggest obstacles to achieving your destiny is giving up too early. How do you stay connected to your destiny and purpose when circumstances are hard? I believe that is probably the greatest game-changer in your journey with God and in life. The greatest way to overcome the obstacle is to identify the problem. If opposition is coming because of something you need to let go of, then start with forgiveness. If you find yourself trying to solve a problem in your own strength, then ask: Am I relinquishing this to God or trying to do it myself?

A few keys will help us stay connected in hard times. One is breaking away to pray and ask God for wisdom. I work out, ride my bike, and talk to God. This has allowed me to hear some really cool things from Him during some of the craziest times in my life. Sometimes I listen to inspirational music and hear God through that. Sometimes I go for walks. When we carve out time for God, He carves out time for us.

Another key is having deep conversations with friends and family.

Having trusted counselors is extremely helpful. The people you allow into your heart and headspace should bring you strength. This does not always necessarily mean you agree with each other; real strength is found in transparency, honest feedback, and the ability to trust that that person has no other agenda than to help you in your search for answers and peace. Being engaged in the connection is very meaningful—being present in the conversation and not looking past them or listening around them. Being engaged involves deep listening and asking meaningful questions.

One of the things God has been weaning out of me is having a hot temper, blowing up and making a scenario bigger than it is, or making assumptions about a person or situation either without hearing all the details or reacting to them in a way I would not want someone else to react if I was the one who made the mistake. God also is teaching me how to communicate well when I disagree with something or someone (because we all feel we are right). Instead of pushing these feelings down and suppressing them, or trying to force others to feel the same way we do, the greatest thing we can do is identify ways to be verbal and open when something bothers us—to have maturity and poise when expressing our opinions. We don't have to be insulting or divisive to share our opinion. Many times, others won't fully subscribe to your point of view or feelings about certain topics. However, we can still grow in our ability to have healthy dialogue in disagreement. If we are able to do that, that's when we are on a course to discovering what real identity, truth, and maturity look like in our personal lives and for those around us.

One other powerful thing we can do to stay connected when circumstances flare up is to declare God's promises over our lives. Isaiah 55:11 says,

> So shall My word be that goes forth from My mouth;
> It shall not return to Me void,
> But it shall accomplish what I please,
> And it shall prosper *in the thing* for which I sent it.

His Word is true, and when we speak it out, it accomplishes things! It also centers our hearts when we are feeling misaligned or sideways in life.

God has a destiny for you, and He is watching over it. He wants it to happen more than you do. God is speaking over you, He has a good plan for you, a good future for you. He wants to be found by you and connect you to a greater purpose. His desire is for us to have peace even in the midst of the storms and tribulations in our lives. Life will be difficult at times, that is a fact. In fact, God's Word says so specifically in John 16:33:

> "These things I have spoken to you, that in Me you may
> have peace. In the world you will have tribulation; but
> be of good cheer, I have overcome the world."

These are all promises that God speaks over us. And they aren't just words in a book; they are promises that God speaks over our lives continually. So one of the things I do when things get hard is to declare these things over my life. Does it immediately alleviate hardship? Sometimes. Does it immediately make the problem go away? Sometimes. Most of the time it doesn't, but it helps me to navigate through the circumstance with a sense of hope. It also establishes a healthy pattern of consistent core values in my life during trying times and empowers me to equip others to establish core values and principles they can rely on when they are struggling, too.

These keys will help us establish our true level of strength when we are being tested. We can have confidence knowing that some of the things we have done, or the circumstances we find ourselves in, are not going to overpower us. We can have peace, even in the midst of chaos, that these promises of Heaven can become a greater reality when circumstances are hard around us or within us.

Keys to Your Destiny: Overcoming the Fear of Man
When I first started following Jesus, I lived in a small town. I was

known there for being very closed off and very disconnected even from my own family. So when I first gave my life to Jesus, I went home and declared it. Then people started to watch me a lot more closely because they were trying to pick apart the Gospel of Jesus, to see if it was real or not in my life (or just in general). They will watch you to see if there is truly transformation in your life. At times people have a true encounter but fall back into their old ways, causing much damage to themselves and those around them because often, the only exposure people have to hope of a redeemed, transformed, and repaired life is through the people who actually receive it, embrace it, and model for them authentically.

Early on, I pressured myself because I knew that—but it was not for me to carry that burden. I had to be careful not to base my growth on what other people were saying or thinking about me. I had to base it on being fully submitted to God.

The first thing I had to do was to repair a reputation that I had developed for myself of being a closed-hearted recluse with a big temper. All that had to be rewired. Prior to my relationship with Christ, I was not married to my wife. That brought a whole other ordeal because I didn't know how to be a husband. All my male role models growing up were absent, so I didn't have any foundation to build upon.

When I gave my life to Jesus, I went on a mission to serve God. In focusing on serving Him and loving people, the Lord gave me a revelation of how to become a better companion to my lady, who would go on to become my wife. It also prompted me to become the best dad I could be to my children, and lastly to contribute to society by helping others discover the way, truth, and purpose for their lives.

So I inherited that new mindset and began serving and building the community. In the process, I started to gain a great new reputation. Not only was I serving the community by being the head coach of the boys basketball team in that town, but I was doing major projects in Nigeria every summer.

Things in our small town were starting to blossom and everything was looking up. We had a community built in (family was there, grandparents, etc.). I had a steady job, as did my wife. Things were really comfortable. Then I got an opportunity to uproot our family and move to California. I decided to pursue the opportunity because I felt like that was the environment we needed to grow in.

Immediately, I got a lot of pushback from my family. I got a lot of people tearing me down. I got a lot of people who I thought were close to me backbiting and saying very horrible and despicable things about me. I always hoped that family would be supportive, no matter what, but in this case we found the opposite. It left a really bad taste in my mouth about family—especially since I hadn't had a strong example of one growing up in the first place.

The circumstances challenged my thinking about what family was supposed to be, but I was still fully committed to what God wanted to do through my life. He gave me a clear revelation of what He wanted to do in the next season, and it didn't include appeasing my wife's family, my family, or even myself. Making the move was the only way to access the things that God had for me and my family—including the extended family.

It was scary. It was a leap of faith. But it helped me hone my focus on loving God and loving the process, and building out from there.

Walking with the Lord is often lonely. The deeper you go with God, the less stuff you can take with you in regard to your own thinking, your own rationale, and your own understanding. The deeper you go with God, the less things might make sense to others. You will feel different inside.

That time, I had to draw a line in the sand and say that I was committed to Jesus and He was going to be the epicenter of my entire life, that my family was going to be founded in Him. My future was going to be founded in Him. Our future was going to be found in Him. God gave me the revelation about moving. But He didn't give it to anyone else around me, so I was responsible for it. No one else was responsible to believe it; I was.

Keys to Your Destiny: Ask as Much as You Want
When we start to waver, we need to take that right to God. Ask as much as you want! Every time circumstances get hard, we have to bring them back to God. If we remember we are doing things to serve Him, we do not have to attach the outcomes to ourselves. We just need to ask Him to let us know if we are off track. The second question we should ask is: "Are people around me greater and stronger because of this decision?"

You want to ask yourself if you are growing in favor with both God and man. Sometimes, the favor of God goes before the favor of man. It's your job to reflect the favor of God to people and help them understand that it's obtainable for them as well. When you reflect that favor, calling, and grace, it invites them to grow. More importantly, it offers them hope that darkness does not have to consume their lives.

As you grow, you'll start to see growth in the people around you. That's what happened with my family. I started following God, and my family followed right along. I think they saw that I was serious and that I was not going to compromise the Gospel, the calling, or the revelation that God had given me. I was all in at any cost— including their opinions about me.

My family started to trust my perspective more because they saw I was consistent in what I was saying, what I was believing, and how I was acting. They saw I was communicating better and that I had more joy and peace even in the midst of conflict or disagreement. They saw I was not trying to convert people, box them in, or make them believe as I did. Instead, I would just reflect the grace of God that saved me and tell people they could have that grace, peace, and joy, too.

To stay on track in your destiny, you always want to ask yourself, "Is this going to help people grow while it's helping me grow? Is this going to make people around me better? Not just my family but people from all walks of life—men, women, children, families, single moms, fatherless children, single dads. Is this going to help?"

Keys to Your Destiny: Make Mistakes
Toxic, unhealthy religion is man's attempt to attain perfection. Religion requires you to fake it and pretend you are something you are not (i.e., perfect). Many of us have been hurt when we see religious people who are not all they profess to be, but the truth is, they never could be all those things. Unhealthy religion is man's attempt to be like God. We see many people in the Bible who made mistakes. God never tries to hide that from us, but shows us how we can be redeemed despite it. He shows us He does not judge us for it. He did for a certain time period; however, Jesus came and took that judgment for us. And we have access to that redemption in Him.

We can grow tremendously in a sense of destiny and purpose when we know it is OK to not get it right all the time. It is so much healthier to own it than to fake it. When you own your mistakes, you offer hope and truth to others and yourself! Give yourself some slack to grow in your journey with God. It doesn't have to all go smoothly for it to all be good and redeemable. When you are doing really well, how many people are you helping navigate their challenges, and how many are you pulling up to your level of hope? Fulfillment happens when we help others discover the same thing.

Daniel had a spirit of excellence about him. The king had governors and many other wise people around him, but the Bible says Daniel set himself apart because there was an "excellent spirit" about him. He was excellent in what he did. I'm not perfect in what I do, but I try to be as excellent as possible.

In trying to be excellent, you're going to fail. You're going to make mistakes. But excellence is also how you handle mistakes and defeat, how you handle apologizing, how you care for other people's hearts when you mess up and it impacts them. That is excellence.

Growing up, I was never taught that it was OK to make mistakes. I thought I had to be perfect to make up for the flaws that pushed my dad away. These were all lies that I was being told by the enemy— that I had pushed my dad away, that I made my mom resentful toward me or angry with me, which pushed me out of the house at an early age. These things were all lies that were trying to get me to adopt a lifestyle that would be destructive for me.

My sense of destiny came out of going on that journey with the Lord, admitting, "I don't have it all together," and just being open and transparent about that.

When you know what God says about you according to His Word, it alleviates the pressure of having to figure it out on your own. You have the Holy Spirit; the Bible calls Him a "counselor." You have the Holy Spirit to ask for wisdom and guidance on what to do next, how to resolve the situation, grow from it, and impact people by the way you respond to your own mistakes, shortcomings, and failures.

Keys to Unlocking Your Destiny: Choose What is Lifegiving
Deuteronomy 30:19 says,

> "I call heaven and earth as witnesses today against you, *that* I have set before you life and death, blessing and cursing; therefore choose life, that both you and your descendants may live."

What does it mean to "choose life"?

As human beings, we want to have all the answers before we make a decision. Following God, or even just starting a relationship with the Lord, is really yielding as opposed to knowing. When you submit yourself to the Lord and discover your destiny and what God says about you, you start to come into the inheritance of your purpose and to feel more alive.

You give life to others when you see the good in them even when they make mistakes and fail. This is what God does for you. When I used to work kid camps for the Seattle Supersonics, I was known as a coach who was always encouraging. I would encourage kids out loud.

Sometimes, they would make a bad play, and I'd say, "That's okay. We still love you as a team. You're doing great. Keep it going." I was calling out the gold in the midst of their shame. I was saying things that would bring life to places where shame would like to kill and destroy them.

When we say yes to God, He starts to call out the gold in our lives openly. In the midst of our shame, in the midst of our guilt, in the midst of our hiccups, in the midst of our triumphs, He calls us out with encouragement. When you give people hope in the midst of their turmoil, they come into a greater revelation of who God is to them. They come into a greater understanding of who they are in Him. They believe they can get through things; they can work hard, they can grow and dust the dirt off their lives and continually move forward.

What does having a sense of destiny and purpose do for people? It helps us feel empowered, it helps us feel like we have options and hope. Whether we come from a small town, a fatherless home, an abusive home, or just feel unseen and unvalued, when we know we're championed not only by God, but by people, we feel like we can accomplish more, that we can accomplish anything. We feel free. We feel empowered. We feel loved, affirmed, strengthened, grounded.

We feel like we have a foundation we can build upon. Something stable even when we fall. A life of faith can simply start with a life of prayer. If you don't have a prayer life, you can start one by sitting down and simply talking to God. Everyone wants to feel loved, and everyone desires to feel known and valued. Prayer is a great entry point for those things.

Our sense of destiny and purpose as believers and followers of Jesus allows us to transport His presence in our lives wherever we go. We get the incredible opportunity to bring the Kingdom of God and champion others along the way. Then they come to a greater understanding, a greater revelation of what is possible for them. It gives them a greater sense of hope and purpose—a sense of what they're designed to inherit, reflect, and release in society.

There's nothing more powerful and freeing for us than coming into our identity and destiny and propelling others into theirs. Psalms 49:11 says that the dwelling places for the next generations are the things we help them build. These are things like their thought life, their hearts, what they know to be true, and how they know God to be true to them.

Psalms 145:4 says, "One generation shall praise Your works to another, and shall declare Your mighty acts." When I got the chance to go back to my small town and coach after my professional athletic career ended, parents and some of the kids I used to coach wanted to talk with me. A lot of them would say how much I had impacted their lives—how since that time many of them had started families and were raising their kids based on what I taught them. What??!!! That was only because I was submitted to God in the process, and committed to calling out what He had in store for their lives.

I wasn't even necessarily sharing the Gospel with them, at least in how I thought it was supposed to be shared at the time. I would just spend time and listen to them, give them a place to be open.

Oftentimes, that would lead to giving them a word of advice or encouraging them that they could be who they wanted to be. They could achieve what they wanted if they were submitted to the process.

When you infuse that in a young person, you infuse them with hope. It's almost like putting rocket fuel in a missile. You infuse them with super-charged revelation, confidence, identity, and vision of what they can accomplish with their lives. One of the kids I coached when he was in the ninth grade told me he wanted to be a commercial airline pilot. So I decided to encourage and champion him in that. He would talk about it a lot. It wasn't just a whimsical dream that he just threw out there. No, this was something he really wanted to do!

Several years later, I returned to that town for a brief visit and bumped into that boy's dad. He told me his son went on to be a commercial airline pilot. Not only that, but he was a flight instructor for other commercial pilots—he became that good. I couldn't tell you how proud I was. I was probably prouder than his own dad, because I remembered all those conversations with him about his dreams. This was what he wanted to do with his life, and I told him as a young kid, "You're going to do it, believe in that. Believe God has a plan for your dream."

Keys to Unlocking Your Destiny: Don't Disqualify Yourself
Jeremiah 1:6–7 says,

> Then said I:
> "Ah, Lord GOD!
> Behold, I cannot speak, for I *am* a youth."
> But the LORD said to me:
> "Do not say, 'I *am* a youth,'
> For you shall go to all to whom I send you,
> And whatever I command you, you shall speak."

We humans tend to disqualify ourselves before giving God a

chance to qualify us. Jeremiah tried to disqualify himself for being too young. God told him, "Don't say that! You are serving Me, and I will help you! Don't say 'I can't do this.' Don't say, 'I don't have any understanding of that.'"

For example, I am not qualified to write this book—but here I am doing it because God called me to it. In Him, when we feel we aren't qualified, that makes us qualified! When we are weak, He is strong. Strange, but very true! The fact that you are reading this is an example of how God can qualify us all for what He has called us to do, even when we can't see it.

One of the greatest privileges we get as followers of Jesus Christ is to be who He has designed us to be. We see this in Romans 12:2, which tells us, "Do not be conformed to this world, but be transformed by the renewing of your mind, that you may prove what *is* that good and acceptable and perfect will of God."

We can't be conformed to this world. We can't allow this world to write the narrative for us. Instead, we align ourselves with what has already been paid for on the cross; the renewing of our mind, the renewing of our heart and spirit comes by submitting to God. Testing is a part of that. In that testing, you start to develop discernment about what's good and what's not. You start to develop oneness with God and learn to lead others from that oneness.

When we're at one with God, we are protected. When we fully abandon ourselves to Him, that means we are fully letting go of what this world is telling us about how we should think, what we should think, what we should believe, and how that should dictate the narrative that is being written over our lives.

It doesn't mean you're careless and ignore the truth. It means you're so anchored in the truth that God qualifies you to reflect light to the world in the midst of the chaos. When you know your purpose in God, it allows you to be that light. I love what Matthew 5:13 says:

"You are the salt of the earth; but if the salt loses its flavor, how shall it be seasoned? It is then good for nothing but to be thrown out and trampled underfoot by men."

Once you lose your essence of the Kingdom, you basically blend in with everything else in this world. That scripture goes on to say that you are the light of the world, a city set on a hill that cannot be hidden.

We are called to do good works; those good works reflect our purpose and our destiny. That gives glory to our Father in Heaven. Because I didn't know my earthly father, my good works in the very beginning were done to feel accepted, to feel received, to feel admired. I was doing good works to gain people's acceptance and adoration. Little did I know my Heavenly Father was already proud of me. He already accepted me! You are already accepted too! Don't disqualify yourself, but receive the open embrace of God's acceptance and adoration.

Keys to Unlocking Your Destiny: Knowing Your Father

God knows what you need from the very beginning. He knew what I needed. What I thought was a defense mechanism turned into something greater. Remember when I said I would take the greatest attribute of every single man I met and try to emulate it? I did not know it at the time, but I was compiling a representation of my Heavenly Father.

He is kind. He is forgiving. He's funny. He's smart. He's loving. He's embracing. He's steadfast. He's generous. He's wealthy. He's spontaneous. He makes me laugh. He picks me up. He fulfills me. He gives me purpose. He gives me destiny. He gives me a good inheritance and He challenges me to grow into someone greater. He's honest and authentic in His desire to see me mature in my living days. In finding out about all of that, I found my purpose. I established what I wanted with an earthly father, but I got a chance to experience that with my Heavenly Father. You can, too.

Whatever you need, whatever is missing for you, God is more than enough to fill that gap. Not just to fill it, but to make abundant life flow out of that place you thought made you broken, undesirable, and less than.

Your Invitation to Know the Way, the Truth, and the Life

Jesus died to give us access to the best way to go, the truth about ourselves, and the life we long to live. He died to give us access to a greater heavenly environment which this world cannot provide. He died to give us access to a heavenly perspective that this world cannot provide.

He died to give us a way to know what God's will is in any situation, and to be agents of change in the world. Your invitation to live empowered, to live with power to overcome your past and your struggles, is waiting for you. Your invitation into a new life is waiting. You can say yes or no; God will not force Himself into your life.

If you say yes, Jesus becomes Lord and Savior of your life. He's Lord over your thinking. He's Lord over your doubt. He's Lord over your ambitions. He's Lord over your fears, struggles, and successes. He's Lord over everything in your heart so that any time you come into a space or thought, He is Lord in it. That's where He can really start navigating your heart. He starts to help you know what you need to know in order to have purpose, love, and fulfillment. He empowers you to make greater decisions than you knew how to make.

If you say yes, you start a journey of being redeemed and repaired (or as believers say, "saved") and growing in living that way. He offers you, every day, the ability to overcome anything that would try to stop you. He will save you from your past and tell you that it does not dictate your future. He will tell you there is a greater opportunity to change, no matter what your background or circumstance is. All of this is yours, even when you feel that you don't deserve it.

If you say yes, there is also always hope. When things go wrong, there is hope for redemption and purpose. I am tearing up while writing this, thinking of you, wherever you might be, because my desire is that you discover this life-changing hope for yourself. Whatever we have been through, God does not want to give us just deep healing, but also fresh understanding and revelation for the life He has for us, where He wants us to go, and how we can get there.

God's will is that you would have a life full of abundance, hope, and purpose. Abundance means you have a full measure of His presence in your life, even when things aren't going well. Hope is the expectation of good even when things are tough. Purpose is walking fulfilled and helping others to do the same. If you have Christ, and His perspective, you start to become the one who impacts your environment. You start to see that you have a greater ability to impact mindsets and hearts and help shape healthy environments, not based on what you can do, but because of Who lives inside your heart and mind daily.

Wherever you go, when you have Jesus with you the environment does not have to knock you off a healthy, empowered course for your life. You actually become the one to impact the environment and shift the culture wherever you are. You can be the one to shift the surroundings wherever you step. That is incredible news!

This invitation is extended to all, but it only becomes powerful to change your life when you accept it, embrace it, and start to live it each and every day, even when it's tough. When you say yes to that invitation, you start to really see the way to go and the truth about yourself. The empowered life that you were meant to live starts to become completely possible! You can walk in the Way, Truth, and Life that you were destined to live. I am so excited for the endless opportunities, freedom, and joy that accompany His love. I pray that you see His daily invitation and partner with it every time. In doing so you will see the way, the truth, and the life become a reality all your living days.

Bless you.

CPSIA information can be obtained
at www.ICGtesting.com
Printed in the USA
JSHW051111140123
36082JS00007B/18